Beware: How The System Breaks You by Subjugating Your Wife or Partner

A Novel by

Wilfried S. Graf von Gerechtberg

Email Address: gm-d@gmx.de

Translated by

TopMeilleurs

© 2024 **Wilfried S. Graf von Gerechtberg**. All rights reserved. No part of this book may be reproduced, distributed, or transmitted in any form or by any means, including photocopying, recording, or other electronic or mechanical methods, without the prior written permission of the author.

TABLE OF CONTENTS

Dedication vii

Prologue ix

PART 1: Assassination Attempts 1

    Chapter 1: Leo, a Target to Eliminate 2

    Chapter 2: Accidents Suspected but Unproven 8

    Chapter 3: Frustrating Failures for the Criminals 12

    Chapter 4: Leo Survives, But Remains in Danger 15

PART 2: Trapping the Wife 19

    Chapter 1: The Decision to Use Eva 20

    Chapter 2: The Appearance of the Agent Romeo 24

    Chapter 3: Seduction and Deceptive Promises 28

    Chapter 4: Eva: Trapped and Enslaved 32

PART 3: A Woman Under Control 37

    Chapter 1: The Blackmail of Compromising Videos 38

    Chapter 2: Eva's Double Life 42

    Chapter 3: Emotional Detachment from Leo 46

    Chapter 4: Eva, a Powerless Puppet 49

PART 4: Eva's Mission: Driving Leo to Suicide 54

    Chapter 1: The Criminals' Orders: Breaking Leo Psychologically 55

    Chapter 2: Eva, the Unwilling Instrument of Destruction 60

    Chapter 3: The Mental Torture Orchestrated by Eva 65

    Chapter 4: Leo's Struggle Against Growing Depression 70

PART 5: Making Leo Appear Insane 75
    Chapter 1: A New, More Insidious Strategy 76
    Chapter 2: Gradual Discrediting 80
    Chapter 3: Subtle Psychological Manipulations 87
    Chapter 4: Leo Begins to Doubt His Mental Health 91

PART 6: The Shadows Deepen 96
    Chapter 1: Leo senses a change, without understanding it 97
    Chapter 2: Eva becomes more distant and absent 101
    Chapter 3: Leo fails to notice the signs of manipulation 104
    Chapter 4: The criminal network tightens its grip 107

PART 7: The Psychological Decline of Leo 111
    Chapter 1: Leo loses confidence in himself 112
    Chapter 2: Troubling events and subtle manipulations 115
    Chapter 3: Eva plays her role despite herself 118
    Chapter 4: Leo struggles to understand what is happening 121

PART 8: Love Turned Into a Weapon 125
    Chapter 1: Eva Becomes the Instrument of Leo's Destruction 126
    Chapter 2: The Orders She Must Follow 129
    Chapter 3: Leo Feels the Unease but Doesn't Understand 133
    Chapter 4: A Toxic Romantic Dynamic 135

PART 9: The Progressive Suffocation 139
    Chapter 1: The manipulation grows increasingly intense 140
    Chapter 2: Leo Tries to Hold on to His Reality 144
    Chapter 3: Eva's lies spiral out of control 149
    Chapter 4: The descent into darkness accelerates 155

PART 10: The Invisible Network 159
Chapter 1: The Puppet Masters Pulling the Strings 160
Chapter 2: Eva Under Complete Control 163
Chapter 3: Leo Increasingly Isolated 166
Chapter 4: The Imminence of the Breaking Point 169

PART 11: The Brutal Awakening 175
Chapter 1: Leo Discovers Troubling Clues 176
Chapter 2: The Truth About the Assassination Attempts Emerges . 179
Chapter 3: Eva: Both Victim and Accomplice 183
Chapter 4: The Inevitable Confrontation 186

PART 12: Devastating Truths 190
Chapter 1: The Compromising Videos of Eva 191
Chapter 2: Leo Confronted with the Ultimate Betrayal 194
Chapter 3: The Combination of the Network's Destructive Interactions 198
Chapter 4: Leo on the Brink of Collapse 202

PART 13: The Fall of Leo 207
Chapter 1: Leo Facing His Mental Destruction 208
Chapter 2: Eva, Torn Between Guilt and Submission 212
Chapter 3: Relationship Shattered Forever 215
Chapter 4: The Choice Between Vengeance and Despair 219

PART 14: The Manipulators Exposed 224
Chapter 1: The true masterminds behind the conspiracy 225
Chapter 2: The criminal network revealed 230
Chapter 3: Eva was just a puppet 233
Chapter 4: The quest for justice or revenge 237

PART 15: The Final Revelation 241
   Chapter 1: The discovery of the final elements of the conspiracy .. 242
   Chapter 2: The invisible ramifications 245
   Chapter 3: Leo faces his destiny 250
   Chapter 4: The ultimate choice 253

PART 16: On the Ruins of Truth 258
   Chapter 1: Leo After the Storm 259
   Chapter 2: Eva, a Broken but Freed Woman 263
   Chapter 3: Surviving the Horror of Truth 268
   Chapter 4: The Uncertainty of the Future 272

Epilogue 276

Dedication

To all the silent victims of moral persecution and harassment, to those who endure the insidious violence of criminal groups without ever finding justice, because the laws lack the effectiveness and will to provide real support. This book is for you, who silently bear the injustice of passive complicity, allowing these persecutions to persist. May your courage and resilience never be forgotten.

With the hope that in a world where technology can detect even the slightest signs of threat, the priority will finally be to protect the most vulnerable, to identify and put an end to these criminal activities that too often escape the radar of authorities.

To the women, wives, and daughters who are used and turned into weapons against those they love, victims themselves of a cycle of manipulation and threats. To you, who carry invisible burdens and face impossible choices, may this book stand as a testament to your suffering and your courage.

May this book serve an educational and preventive purpose, opening eyes and minds, so these stories no longer repeat themselves and justice is finally served. You are the reason for these pages, the strength behind every word.

PROLOGUE

Dear Reader,

In the quiet moments of life, when you look into the eyes of the person who shares your heart, it is easy to believe that love will carry you through anything. But what if the very system you trust to protect and support you silently and systematically eroded the foundation of your relationship? What if the pressures imposed on your partner, the one you vowed to cherish, slowly and insidiously tore apart the fabric of your bond?

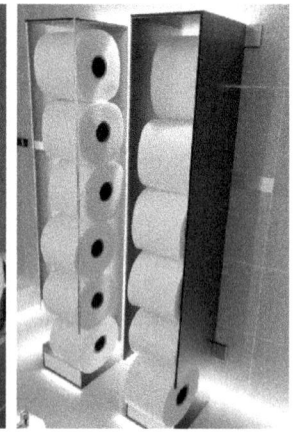
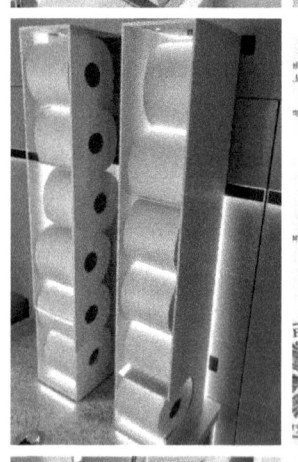
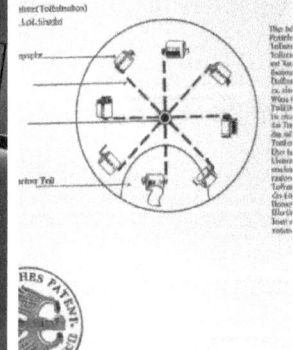

PART 1:

Assassination Attempts

Chapters:

1. Leo, a Target to Eliminate

2. Suspected but Unproven Accidents

3. Frustrating Failures for the Criminals

4. Leo Survives but Remains in Danger

CHAPTER 1:

Leo, a Target to Eliminate

L eo gazed out over Berlin from his office window, a mixture of admiration and anxiety in his heart. This city, which had seen him grow up, had never truly accepted the idea that a man of foreign origin could embody such success. The son of immigrants, he still carried the invisible weight of others' gaze. Despite his intelligence, perseverance, and deep desire to integrate into German society, Leo remained the foreigner in the eyes of many, someone who was never truly "one of them."

Unlike the American dream, where every effort is supposed to lead to success, the "German dream" seemed to elude people like Leo, no matter their merit. In Germany, succeeding while coming from elsewhere often seemed to be viewed as a cruel irony, almost an implicit violation of social rules. Yet, he had overcome all these obstacles. At 42, he was now a respected man, a visionary engineer with revolutionary ideas in the field of renewable energy. His patents, involving technologies that could change the game, were internationally recognized.

However, behind this apparent success, a silent threat loomed, invisible but imminent. Despite his ability to anticipate technical problems in his field, Leo couldn't see the trap closing around him. Married to Eva, who was also of foreign origin, and father of three children, he had everything to be happy. But it was all just a deceptive facade.

The first assassination attempts had begun several months ago. Leo, rational and down-to-earth, hadn't recognized them for what they were. It had started with incidents he had labeled as accidents or bad luck: a car that nearly collided with him as he drove down a mountain road, or scaffolding that collapsed on a construction site, just inches from him. Each time, he found logical explanations. But he hadn't perceived the malicious intent behind them.

What he didn't know was that his success had drawn the attention of criminal networks operating in the shadows of the German economy. These groups, well entrenched in the country's economic structures, saw his innovations as a direct threat to their established interests.

Leo, unknowingly, had destabilized colossal interests by promoting technologies that could disrupt energy and economic monopolies. To them, he wasn't just a successful entrepreneur; he was an enemy to be eliminated.

They initially tried to take him out subtly. Accidents disguised as misfortunes were their method of choice: more discreet, they left few traces and aroused little suspicion. But Leo, a man of science, refused to believe that his life was in danger. He thought that his success spoke for him, and that his inventions could only inspire admiration and respect. However, behind the scenes, the opposing forces, those who feared the disruption of their hegemony, saw him in a different light.

A man of foreign origin with overly revolutionary ideas was a catalyst for change they couldn't tolerate. He was a breaker of the status quo. His success made them feel that they were losing control, that their power was being eroded by a foreigner who challenged the established order. In their minds, Leo was the embodiment of what they feared: an outsider who disrupted the system and questioned their dominance.

What they hadn't anticipated, however, was Leo's resilience. He had grown up in adversity, the child of immigrants who had fled poverty to build a new life in Germany. This inner strength, forged by years of struggling to be accepted in a society that marginalized him, would be his asset against those who sought to bring him down. However, for the time being, Leo was unaware of the extent of the danger that loomed over him.

Eva, his wife, was becoming increasingly distant, but Leo attributed this to the pressure of work and family worries. What he didn't yet see was that the criminal networks, unable to break him through direct attacks, had already begun to infiltrate his private life. They had decided to go through Eva, not to kill her, but to use her as a weapon against him. Eva had become their next target, not to be eliminated, but to be used as an instrument of psychological destruction.

The assassination attempts had failed. Leo, through almost unconscious survival instinct, had survived each trap laid for him. The criminals were frustrated, but far from giving up. They knew there were other, more insidious ways to destroy a man. They would attack what he held most dear: his family. Where physical violence hadn't worked, they would strike more subtly, on the psychological level. Eva, under pressure and manipulated, would become the most destructive weapon against her own husband.

The criminal network didn't need to kill him directly. The goal was to break him from the inside, to push him to the brink until he lost his footing. Their strategy was clear: emotionally isolate Leo, destroy his trust in those he loved, and push him slowly into the abyss of despair. Every step was calculated, every manipulation orchestrated in the shadows. But Leo, a brilliant engineer but a man of heart, continued to live in the illusion that everything was fine, that things would work out. He didn't know that the greatest threat was coming from within his own home.

Eva, under pressure, would become their weapon. But for that, they had to compromise her, break her moral defenses, and plunge her into a cycle from which she could never escape. An apparently innocent meeting with a charming and seductive man, exchanged confidences, and soon compromising videos would bind her to them forever. What started as a simple conversation would soon transform into an infernal spiral.

Leo, the rational engineer, remained blind to what was happening. To him, the world kept turning normally, even though he sometimes felt anxieties he couldn't explain. The danger was there, lurking in the shadows, waiting for its moment. But Leo, too confident, saw nothing coming. The trap was slowly closing, yet he continued to believe that everything would work itself out.

What Leo didn't know was that the most destructive attacks aren't always the ones that are visible. He was going to be broken, not by a brutal attack, but by a slow erosion of his trust, his certainties, everything he had built. The criminal network knew that a man's true strength lies in those he loves. And that's where they would strike, where Leo was most vulnerable.

CHAPTER 2:

Accidents Suspected but Unproven

Leo, usually so calm and self-assured, had found himself over the past few months facing events that completely overwhelmed him. Accustomed to analyzing everything with the cold logic of an engineer, he struggled to find logical explanations for what was happening to him. He had always refused to believe in bad luck, that abstract notion that seemed to belong to those who couldn't control their fate. But recently, something strange seemed to have befallen him.

"It can't be bad luck," he thought as he drove through the familiar streets of Berlin. **"But then what is it?"**

Each event seemed more troubling than the last. First, the faulty brakes. That had been the first sign. One morning, as he was driving along during rush hour, the brakes on his car had suddenly failed. A surge of panic had overwhelmed him. The pedal, which had always responded with precision, had become unresponsive. Leo had felt his heart race, but with a flash of calm, he managed to pull the handbrake in time. He narrowly avoided colliding with the car in front of him. Death had been only a few centimeters away.

After exiting the car, still short of breath, he had tried to rationalize the situation. Maybe a technical failure? He had had his vehicle checked by a mechanic, but no anomaly had been detected. Nothing that could explain the sudden failure. **"Why is this happening to me now?"** he wondered.

Leo knew Berlin well, its streets, its potential dangers. He wasn't an irresponsible driver, and his car wasn't old. The possibility of sabotage began to cross his mind, but he dismissed it as ridiculous. Who could possibly want to harm him? **"It's probably just a coincidence…"** he repeated to himself, though he didn't truly believe it.

Then, other more troubling events followed, such as the day a car driven by a young woman, Annika H., suddenly tried to corner him in traffic. The memory of that moment still gave him chills. Had Leo given in and changed lanes, he would have certainly crashed under the wheels of a heavy truck. But some instinct he couldn't explain had made him stick to his course. Annika lost control and crashed into an advertising board after driving over a traffic island. An improbable and violent scene.

Leo remembered the dull thud of the impact and the scene that followed: panicked bystanders, indifferent police officers, and that unknown man who rushed forward to shout that he was a witness, insisting that Leo had caused the accident. It all seemed too well orchestrated.

Leo could no longer ignore what was happening: this wasn't an accident. He felt it deep down. The police officers' gazes, their complete lack of questioning at the scene, all of it seemed abnormal. A mechanic later confirmed that the "accident" bore the marks of a premeditated attack, carefully orchestrated. "**But why?**" Leo kept repeating. "**Why me?**"

Despite the evidence, Leo still refused to believe that he was the target of something bigger. But this reality would hit him squarely a few weeks later, with another assassination attempt.

Someone had sabotaged his vehicle, cutting the fuel line and causing a dangerous leak. While he was driving, unaware, a car sped past him, and one of the passengers threw a cigarette butt, hoping the gasoline would catch fire and destroy the car. Leo, still unaware of the danger, continued driving until a motorcyclist, an accomplice in the operation, threw another cigarette butt under his vehicle as he stopped at a red light. This time, flames erupted.

Leo still remembered the panic that surged within him when he saw the flames licking the underside of his car. His first reaction was to rush out, leaving behind what could have been his tomb. "It's just an accident…" he tried to convince himself once again, but now he knew that was no longer possible.

Each day, the events became more violent, more dangerous. Leo was beginning to piece together the puzzle: this wasn't a simple coincidence. He was a target, and those who wanted him dead would stop at nothing to achieve their goal. Yet, despite the mounting evidence, he still didn't know who was behind it all or why.

Why me? What do they want? These questions haunted him more and more each day. Leo lived in constant confusion and anxiety because, although he was beginning to understand the scope of the threat, he still couldn't fully grasp who his adversaries were. But he knew something terrible was brewing in the shadows, and he could no longer afford to ignore it.

CHAPTER 3:

Frustrating Failures for the Criminals

The criminals, though used to operating in the shadows with tactics of manipulation and violence, were facing an unexpected obstacle: Leo's endurance. All the attempts to eliminate him had repeatedly failed, plunging the network into growing frustration. Their initial plan had seemed solid. They had orchestrated accidents with methodical precision, hoping these events would end Leo's life without raising suspicion. But each time, Leo outsmarted their expectations with his resilience.

One of the first significant failures was the defective brake incident. When Leo managed to avoid disaster by pulling the handbrake at the last second, the criminals realized they couldn't solely rely on classic methods to achieve their goal. Then, the sabotage of the fuel line, which could have caused a fatal fire, also failed. This series of failures only fueled their hatred and obsession to destroy him.

Another event, involving Annika H., marked a turning point in their strategies. Contrary to what Leo thought, Annika had never lost control of her vehicle accidentally. The entire incident had been carefully planned to force Leo into making hasty decisions and trigger his downfall. If Leo had changed lanes, he would have collided with a truck. But by refusing to yield, he outsmarted the network. Frustrated but determined, Annika veered her vehicle into a traffic island, triggering a voluntary accident with a billboard, hoping the incident would lead to accusations against Leo.

The network had planned everything: the accomplice, a fake witness who was supposed to point the finger at Leo as the cause of the accident, as well as corrupt police officers ready to falsify the report. But once again, Leo escaped their trap. His photos of the scene and his precise testimony exposed the witness's lies. This complex maneuver failed, leaving the criminals not only frustrated but increasingly exposed to the possibility of being uncovered.

Each failure cracked their strategy, and they came to the conclusion that physical attacks would not be enough. Leo had shown a tenacity that surpassed their expectations. It was then that they decided to change their tactic, no longer aiming to destroy him physically, but psychologically. The idea was simple: break Leo from within.

To do this, they would target the person who meant the most to him: Eva, his wife. They knew that by manipulating the one who shared his life, they could reach him more deeply, where he would be most vulnerable. They were setting the stage for a much more insidious attack, a plan designed to make Leo lose all emotional and mental stability, eroding his confidence and gradually cutting him off from his reality.

This strategy would require additional resources and careful planning. The network knew that it was no longer just a matter of eliminating him, but of destroying him from the inside, slowly, until he was nothing but a shadow of his former self. It was a game of patience, where every strike had to be delivered with precision, every manipulation carefully calibrated to push him to the limit.

Thus began a new phase in the silent war waged against Leo, a phase where physical violence gave way to emotional and psychological violence of a terrifying intensity.

CHAPTER 4:

Leo Survives, But Remains in Danger

Leo had survived several mysterious incidents, but a growing anxiety haunted him. He didn't understand why these events kept happening around him or why he always emerged unscathed, though deeply disturbed. A man of logic, Leo refused to believe in mere coincidence. The thought that someone might be targeting him for no apparent reason crossed his mind, but he had no tangible proof.

Every morning, he woke up with the strange sensation of being watched, hunted, yet unable to fully grasp what was unfolding around him. The accidents, a sudden brake failure, an unexpected fuel leak, even a staged collision attempt, formed a pattern that he could not ignore. Yet, no rational explanation came to ease his fears.

His confusion grew with each new incident. Leo lived in a constant state of vigilance, watching for any sign of danger, but never knowing when or how the next attack would occur. He found himself trapped in a spiral of unanswered questions, increasingly doubting the normality of the events.

His isolation grew as, after each accident, the police dismissed his concerns with a wave of the hand. Despite the evidence he had gathered, photos, testimonies, the authorities saw nothing suspicious. Rational explanations crumbled in the face of this general indifference, plunging Leo into a deeper state of despair. He felt trapped in an invisible web, woven by hands he knew nothing about.

The threat was not only external. At home, Leo no longer felt safe. The growing distance from Eva, his wife, added to his distress. He, who had always believed he could count on her, now felt a barrier between them. His home, once a refuge, had become a place of tension where he could no longer find comfort.

His anxiety fed off this lack of explanation and the silence surrounding him. He wavered between hoping it was just bad luck and fearing that something much darker was at play. This doubt gnawed at him, keeping him in a constant state of stress.

Yet, Leo refused to succumb to panic. He tried to remain strong for his family, but every day, he felt his certainties wobbling a little more.

In his moments of solitude, one thought haunted him: why him? Who could want him dead? He had never been a man who made enemies. Yet, everything pointed to someone, or a group, wanting him out of the game.

Even his interactions with Eva, once full of camaraderie, were now sources of frustration. Eva too seemed to be struggling with an unease she couldn't express. Her emotional distance added to Leo's confusion. Was she also in danger? Or was she part of a game that Leo couldn't access?

As the events unfolded, Leo found himself trapped in a vicious cycle. He remained in danger, that was certain. But how could he fight a threat he didn't fully understand? These assassination attempts disguised as accidents had not yet achieved their goal, but Leo felt that they were just warnings. Something bigger loomed on the horizon. But for now, he was defenseless, alone, and caught in the gears of a machine he could not identify

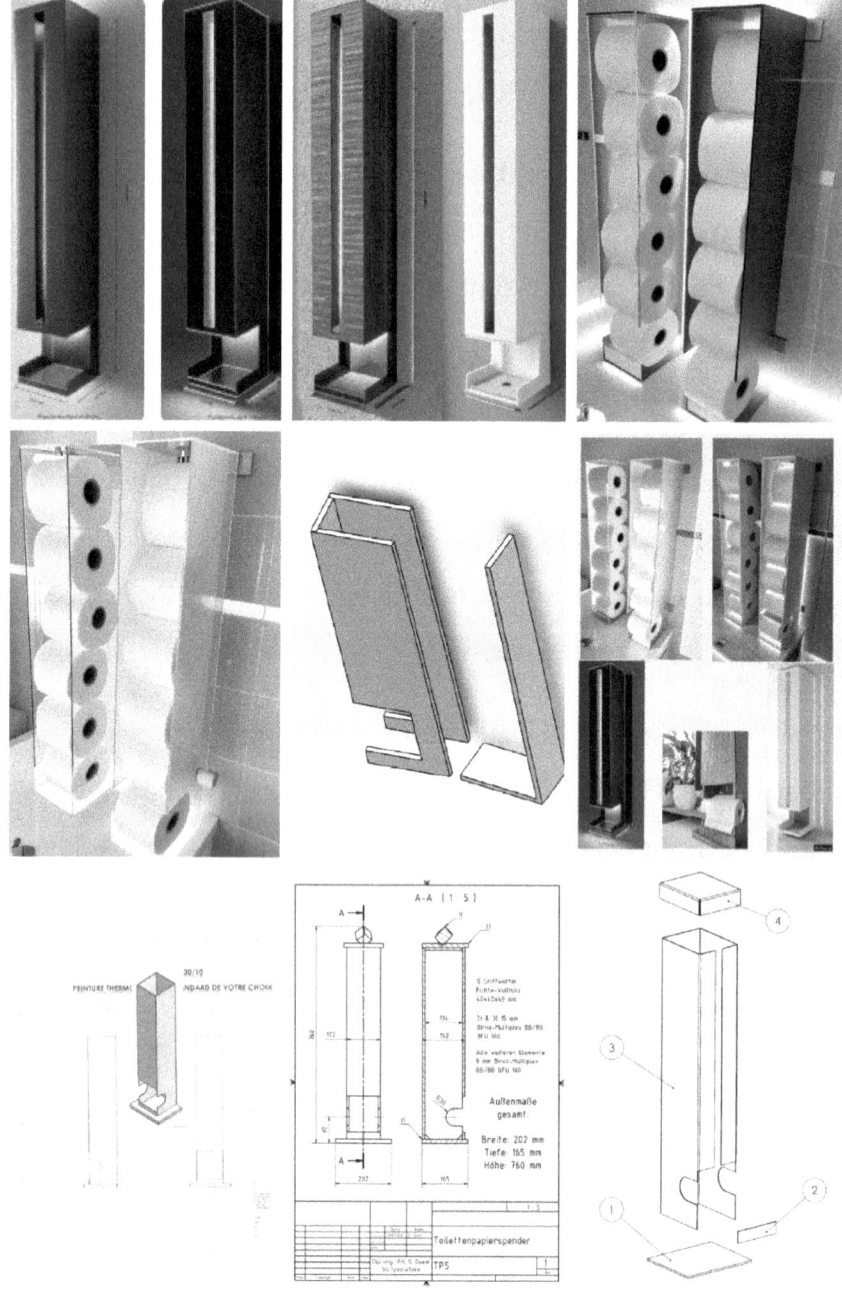

PART 2:

Trapping the Wife

Chapters:

1. The Decision to Use Eva

2. The Appearance of a Agent Romeo

3. Seduction and False Promises

4. Eva, Trapped and Subjugated

CHAPTER 1:

The Decision to Use Eva

In the shadows, the criminal network was reorganizing. The assassination attempts against Leo had failed, fueling the network's growing frustration. Their initial plan to eliminate Leo physically had not worked, as he had always managed to escape just in time, thanks to his survival instinct and mental resilience. These failures meant they had to change their approach. Directly targeting Leo wasn't working, so they needed to find another vulnerability in his life to destroy him from the inside. The network knew Leo was emotionally vulnerable. They decided to target the person closest to him: Eva, his wife.

Eva, with her gentle nature and insecurities, quickly became the ideal target for the network. Far from being a strong and independent woman, she was shy, lacked self-confidence, and carried emotional burdens related to her foreign origins. She was, in short, easily manipulable. The network saw in her not only an opportunity to infiltrate Leo's private life but also to use her own weaknesses against her husband.

The network had not chosen Eva by chance. They had carefully observed the dynamics of her marriage to Leo. Although their relationship appeared solid on the surface, there were cracks, moments of distance and emotional fatigue. Leo, preoccupied with his business and inventions, no longer paid her the same attention as at the beginning of their relationship. The network knew that if someone could penetrate this gap, they would have a chance to break Leo psychologically. It was at this moment that they decided to recruit a very special agent: Jürgen, the Agent Romeo.

The Appearance of the Agent Romeo

Jürgen was chosen carefully to seduce Eva. He was a charismatic, manipulative, and methodical man. His goal was not only to charm Eva but to make her completely dependent on him, to dominate her emotionally, and to use her to reach Leo. The network had already employed this method in similar cases, often to orchestrate divorces or financial manipulations.

From the beginning, Jürgen played his role with cold precision. He approached Eva during a seemingly accidental encounter. Beneath his kind demeanor, Jürgen hid a calculating mind, and every gesture, every word was a maneuver designed to infiltrate Eva's life. He was charming, attentive, and, most importantly, he offered her the listening ear and attention that Leo no longer gave her. Eva, weary of her husband's apparent indifference, was easily seduced.

Seduction and Manipulation

Very quickly, their light and friendly conversations transformed into more intimate encounters. Jürgen mastered the art of seduction, and in no time, Eva became emotionally and physically dependent on him. Gifts, romantic dinners, delicate attentions, everything was orchestrated to make her captive of this new relationship. She felt loved, desired, listened to, everything she thought she had lost with Leo.

But Jürgen did not settle for simple gestures. Gradually, he introduced a more insidious element into their relationship: emotional blackmail. He convinced Eva to record some of their intimate moments, presenting it as a harmless game, a way to strengthen their bond. Eva, eager to please Jürgen and keep his affection, agreed. But what began as a simple "game" quickly transformed into a powerful weapon against her.

The Descent into Submission

With these compromising videos in hand, Jürgen exerted total control over Eva. She was now trapped. The fear that these images would be revealed to Leo paralyzed her. She saw no way out and became completely subjugated by Jürgen and the network. She obeyed their orders without question, terrified of losing everything she had built with Leo. Jürgen even delivered her to other members of the network, exploiting her vulnerability to satisfy their fantasies. Eva had become their slave, both emotionally and physically.

As for Leo, he continued to live in ignorance. He did notice that something had changed with his wife: she was more distant, more reserved, but he attributed it to the tensions of daily life. He never could have imagined that Eva was being used against him, manipulated by a criminal network. His intuition betrayed him, and he had no idea that the danger was no longer only external, but had infiltrated his very home.

Eva's mission was now clear: under the network's orders, she was to drive Leo to depression, madness, and ideally, to suicide. The criminals knew that to destroy Leo, they needed to destroy his mind. Eva, without even fully realizing it, had become the tool of their diabolical scheme.

CHAPTER 2:

The Appearance of the Agent Romeo

The arrival of the Agent Romeo in Eva's life was neither accidental nor coincidental. This seducer, carefully chosen by the criminal network, possessed all the qualities needed to infiltrate the life of a woman who seemed fulfilled but was, in reality, fragile. While Leo, absorbed by his work, appeared distant, Eva, increasingly doubtful, had become the perfect target for the network. This couple, which seemed ideal, turned out to be an easy prey for a more subtle and insidious attack.

The approach of the Agent Romeo was meticulously planned. He knew that to succeed, he had to proceed with caution, without raising suspicion. It all began with a carefully orchestrated encounter. One morning, as Eva dropped off their youngest son at daycare, she met this man in his Mercedes S 600 Maybach, a vehicle that projected not only an image of wealth but also power and prestige. Complimenting Eva on her appearance, he quickly disarmed her, and before she even realized it, she had given him her phone number.

The Agent Romeo had exactly what it took to charm Eva at this point in her life. Charming, refined, and ostentatiously wealthy, he represented an escape from the monotony of her daily routine. Unlike Leo, who seemed increasingly absorbed by his professional projects, this man knew how to listen, flatter, and make Eva feel desired. His subtle way of showing interest in her passions and discreetly complimenting her ego awakened a side of her she thought she had lost long ago.

Eva, who had never been a very self-confident woman, felt vulnerable at this particular moment in her life. Her insecurities, especially related to her status as a foreigner in Germany, made her doubt her place in society and in her own marriage. The Agent Romeo skillfully played on these doubts to gain her trust. His impeccable manners and respectful attitude made him the perfect confidant. He knew how to adjust every interaction, every word, to never make her feel uncomfortable. It was an art he mastered perfectly.

The Agent Romeo didn't settle for immediate contact. He cultivated their relationship carefully. Over the weeks, what had started as light conversations evolved into increasingly intimate exchanges. Eva didn't yet perceive him as a threat. This man seemed to provide what Leo, in his professional frenzy, no longer gave her. The Agent Romeo listened, flattered, and, most importantly, offered Eva his full and undivided attention. She gradually allowed herself to be captivated by this new presence in her life.

This seducer carefully manipulated Eva, encouraging her to express her doubts about her marriage with Leo, the boredom she sometimes felt, and her emotional loneliness. These conversations slowly intensified, always without force, always under the guise of kindness. The Agent Romeo knew exactly what strategy to follow. He had to create a gap, imperceptible but very real, between Eva and Leo. He hinted that she deserved better, that she could find emotional refuge away from her now-monotonous daily life.

Once he had gained Eva's trust, he moved on to the next phase of his plan: emotional manipulation. He offered her moments of intimacy away from prying eyes, away from the routine. Little by little, Eva began to feel loved, desired, and she made decisions she would never have considered before. The Agent Romeo, master of manipulation, even suggested that they record their intimate moments under the pretext of "keeping memories." What initially seemed like an innocent game quickly turned into a sordid trap. These videos, which she thought were just a harmless fantasy, would become instruments of blackmail against her.

The Agent Romeo knew that the more Eva compromised herself, the more power he would have over her. Once he had these videos, the trap was set. Eva, who had succumbed to passion, now found herself a prisoner of her own choices. What had started as a passionate and exciting relationship turned into a nightmare. The Agent Romeo, now holding proof of her infidelity, threatened to reveal these videos if she didn't obey his orders. Eva was trapped.

Far from being a mere seducer, the Agent Romeo was acting under the orders of a much larger criminal network. Every action he took, every gesture he made, was part of a plan orchestrated to destroy Leo. At this point, Eva, still in love with her husband, was already caught in a whirlwind of conflicting emotions. She was torn between her love for Leo and her fear of losing everything because of her mistakes. She didn't yet understand that she had become a pawn in a much bigger game, a game in which her own husband would be the ultimate victim.

CHAPTER 3:

Seduction and Deceptive Promises

The seduction orchestrated by Agent Romeo was both sophisticated and cruel, a perfectly executed scheme designed to exploit Eva's emotional vulnerabilities. At this stage, their relationship, though still budding, had already forged an intimate connection, giving Eva the illusion of finding what was missing in her marriage to Leo. But seducing a married woman like Eva, who had never considered infidelity, required far more than fleeting compliments and superficial attentions. It demanded fine manipulation, a game where every gesture and every word was carefully calculated to bind her more tightly to her captor.

Agent Romeo, a master of manipulation, began to weave promises into his seduction. At first, these promises seemed harmless, almost endearing. He spoke with her about dreams of adventure and freedom, far removed from the monotonous routine she shared with Leo. As their meetings continued, the promises grew grander, more fantastical. He vowed to give her a new life, free from family pressures, marital obligations, and the responsibilities of motherhood. They would travel together, build a fresh start where Leo had no place. These promises played directly on the frustrations Eva had silently harbored for years.

Eva, fragile and yearning for recognition, gradually succumbed to these illusions. She began fantasizing about this life with a man who seemed to understand her so completely. He never criticized her, never asked anything of her except to be herself, or so she believed. He offered her a glimpse of escape from her marital troubles, and in her vulnerable state, she began to think he might be the solution to her unhappiness. Agent Romeo's promises gave her an alternative to the life she found dull alongside Leo, and she clung to them desperately.

Agent Romeo knew exactly where to press to deepen his hold over her. His promises of exotic travel and freedom were mere bait. He had no intention of liberating her from her marriage but rather of ensnaring her in a relationship where she would become emotionally and physically dependent on him. Every promise he made was calculated to widen the gap between her and Leo, pulling her further from the reality of her marriage and immersing her in a deceptive dream. He subtly conditioned her to see her husband as an obstacle to her happiness, a man who didn't understand her needs and kept her trapped in a passionless life.

Blinded by lies and manipulation, Eva gradually distanced herself from Leo. Her thoughts were now consumed by the man who made her feel alive. She became more distant, detached in her roles as a wife and mother. Each encounter with Agent Romeo pushed her further into a spiral where the promises of a bright future and unrestrained love pulled her deeper into illusion. The emotional rift between her and Leo widened, leaving him perplexed about what was happening.

The situation became even more unbearable as Eva failed to realize the cage she was walking into. Agent Romeo's promises, though intoxicating, were nothing but lies. He knew that once she was completely under his sway, he could use her as a pawn to further his agenda, which went far beyond a mere illicit love affair. The network he worked for had far darker plans for Leo, and Eva was merely a tool in their scheme.

What initially seemed like a relationship of passion and desire gradually turned into one of control and manipulation. Agent Romeo began orchestrating scenarios where Eva compromised herself further, stolen moments, lies, increasingly significant betrayals. With every step deeper into this toxic relationship, Eva found herself more trapped, where promises of escape and freedom masked an increasingly oppressive reality.

As the promises piled up, Agent Romeo tightened his grip. The further Eva drifted from Leo, the more tied she felt to the man who promised her a better life. Yet deep down, a part of her knew these promises were lies. However, by then, it was too late to turn back. Agent Romeo had seduced her with such skill that she was now ensnared, torn between her role as a wife and her desire to break free from a life she viewed as a prison.

The emotional manipulation and promises of Agent Romeo would soon transform into tools of blackmail. Though Eva was still captivated, she began to see the first cracks in the illusion. But by this point, it was already too late. She was caught in a trap, and each passing day drew her closer to the moment when she would be forced to betray the man she had vowed to love and protect.

CHAPTER 4:

Eva: Trapped and Enslaved

Eva, once an ordinary woman living in the stability of her marriage to Leo, found herself ensnared in an inescapable web woven by Agent Romeo, Jürgen Hauser. What had begun as flattering encounters and a secret affair quickly spiraled into something dark and oppressive. Jürgen, far from being merely a charming lover, had become the ruthless master of her life. Their relationship was no longer built on passion but on domination and submission.

Under Jürgen's control, Eva lost all autonomy. What had started as stolen moments evolved into a waking nightmare. Jürgen was no longer just a seducer; he had become a merciless manipulator, wielding compromising videos as weapons of control. These recordings of their intimate moments were only the beginning. Soon, Jürgen pushed her into increasingly degrading acts. Eva was no longer in a position to refuse, knowing that defiance could mean the destruction of her life and marriage.

The true turning point came when he forced her to have sex with another man, his friend, while being filmed. Eva felt trapped, yet she complied, clinging to the hope that she might still escape. But Jürgen didn't stop there. This first act of submission marked the start of a downward spiral. After one man came two, then three, eventually five, all participating in the filmed humiliations. Every act, captured in detail by the camera, deepened Jürgen's grip on her. Each video added weight to her already crushing burden, and every act of compliance pulled her further into the horror of her situation.

Eva, once strong and independent, had become a pawn for Jürgen to manipulate at will. He handed her over to his friends and colleagues, showing no regard for her feelings or well-being. She was enslaved, not by physical chains but by a web of psychological terror, with the compromising videos serving as a constant threat. She was no longer a person in Jürgen's eyes but an object, a tool in the criminal network's plans.

Guilt consumed Eva at every moment. Each time she met Leo's gaze, her heart filled with shame and fear. She knew Jürgen wouldn't hesitate to destroy her life if she tried to escape. The videos could be leaked at any moment, exposing her betrayal in the worst possible way. Leo would never see her the same way again. Her children, her husband, her home, everything she held dear, would be annihilated if she dared to defy Jürgen.

And yet, she felt powerless. How could she explain to Leo that she had been trapped? How could she make him understand that it all started with a seduction she thought harmless, and now she was caught in a nightmare? Doubts and fear paralyzed her. She was utterly alone in this terror, unable to seek help for fear of everything crumbling around her.

As weeks passed, Eva sank deeper into despair. She grew more distant from Leo, unable to talk to him or confide in him about what she was enduring. Outwardly, she continued to play the role of a wife and mother, masking her pain and humiliation with an appearance of normalcy. But inside, she felt broken, trapped in a body she no longer controlled, obeying orders that disgusted her.

Jürgen Hauser had not only taken over her life, he had utterly destroyed it. Eva was now nothing more than a puppet, enslaved to his desires and those of the network. Her dreams of a better life, an escape from routine, had turned into a living nightmare. She saw no way out.

As Jürgen tightened his hold, Eva felt her world shrink. The chasm between her and Leo widened daily as she became more withdrawn, consumed by fear and shame. Leo, for his part, sensed that something was wrong with Eva but couldn't fathom the extent of the horror she was silently enduring.

Trapped and enslaved, Eva knew there was no turning back. Jürgen had her firmly in his grasp, and the fear of losing everything, her husband, her children, her life, kept her from breaking free of this hell. She had become a puppet, controlled by forces far stronger than her, unable to break the invisible chains holding her captive.

PART 3:

A Woman Under Control

Chapters:

1. The Blackmail of Compromising Videos

2. Eva's Double Life

3. Emotional Detachment from Leo

4. Eva, a Powerless Puppet

CHAPTER 1:

The Blackmail of Compromising Videos

Eva could never have imagined that her affair with Jürgen, Agent Romeo, would lead to such humiliation and terror. What began as a seemingly passionate escape quickly turned into a nightmare controlled by compromising videos. Every intimate moment recorded during their time together, once perceived as harmless play, had become a potent weapon of blackmail. These videos were no longer memories, they were chains binding Eva in a web of manipulation and threats.

The compromising videos became the core of Jürgen's control over Eva, reinforced by the criminal network behind him. Every moment, Eva lived in fear of her phone vibrating with another message from Jürgen, who had shed his mask of benevolence to reveal a cruel and calculated master. His messages were cold and laden with implicit threats. Phrases like, "If Leo finds out..." or "Imagine what your children would think if they saw this..." plunged Eva into an abyss of terror. She knew her entire life could collapse in an instant, all because of those videos she never should have allowed to be recorded.

As the days passed, the threats escalated. It was no longer just about keeping their relationship a secret from Leo; the blackmail intensified. Jürgen began demanding that Eva deliberately sabotage her husband's life. He was no longer content with merely instilling fear of exposure, he pushed her into actions that directly endangered Leo. Eva was forced to spy on Leo, listen in on his professional conversations, and gather confidential information to relay back to Jürgen. On several occasions, Jürgen even compelled her to create conflicts between Leo and his business partners, sowing seeds of discord.

Every day, Eva found herself playing a double game, smiling at Leo while knowing her actions, dictated by Jürgen, were slowly unraveling the life of the man she loved. Her mind was tortured by the dilemma: betray her husband to maintain the façade, or break free from this destructive hold at the risk of losing everything. Fear became an omnipresent force in her life, making any thought of rebellion seem impossible.

The most troubling aspect for Eva was that the videos were no longer a passive threat. Whenever she faltered or attempted to escape Jürgen's control, he would not hesitate to send her a video clip, cruelly reminding her of the power he held over her. The mere sight of those images paralyzed her with shame and despair. She could not fathom the consequences if these videos were ever made public. Leo, her children, her entire family, everything would be destroyed.

Over the weeks, Jürgen refined his methods of domination. It was no longer just about blackmail; it became a deeper form of psychological manipulation. He pushed her into increasingly compromising situations, forcing her to participate in acts she could never have imagined. Each new video strengthened his grip, each fresh humiliation isolating her further. Eva was no longer just the victim of blackmail, she had become a pawn in a larger game of power, where every move pushed her closer to the breaking point.

This blackmail plunged Eva into a spiral of fear and degradation. She felt trapped in a situation she could not escape, unable to find a way out of the tightening grip. The contrast between the woman she once was, strong, loving, with an apparently idyllic family life, and the woman she had become, a puppet enslaved by terror, was unbearable. Yet, despite the shame and self-loathing, Eva continued to play this sordid game, convinced she had no other choice.

On the outside, everything seemed normal. Leo still suspected nothing concrete, though he felt the growing emotional distance between them. But inside, Eva was crumbling under the pressure, acutely aware that even the slightest misstep could bring everything crashing down. Every passing day brought her closer to the moment when it all might unravel.

CHAPTER 2:

Eva's Double Life

Over time, Eva found herself trapped in a downward spiral of lies and manipulation, leading a double life that was slowly destroying her. On one side, she maintained the facade of a loving wife and devoted mother, the woman Leo and their family believed her to be. On the other side, she was enslaved by Jürgen, Agent Romeo, and the criminal network pulling the strings. Each day, she sank deeper into this parallel existence, torn between the demands of her public life and those of her secret one.

At home, Eva did her best to keep up appearances. Her children and Leo could never suspect the storm raging inside her. She woke up each morning, made breakfast, took the kids to school, and smiled at Leo as if everything were normal. Yet, with every buzz of her phone, her heart raced. Jürgen's messages were no longer those of a tender lover; they were cold commands, dictated by the network's relentless need for control. Eva knew her life was no longer her own.

She was forced to carry out increasingly perverse demands, such as provoking arguments with Leo or subtly manipulating his daily life to destabilize him. She had to create tension and doubt without betraying herself. Every confrontation with Leo became unbearable. She could see that he was trying to understand what was happening, attempting to reconnect with the intimacy they once shared. But his efforts only deepened her guilt, and she felt powerless to escape the invisible grip Jürgen held over her.

In public, Eva continued to play the role of the perfect wife and mother. To family friends, everything seemed fine between her and Leo. She attended social events, parent-teacher meetings, and cared for her children with devotion. Yet behind this facade of perfection, Eva was a woman consumed by constant fear, torn between the love she still felt for her family and the oppressive hold of the criminal network controlling her.

The weight of this double life began to take a heavy toll on her mental and emotional health. Eva withdrew into herself, avoiding moments of genuine intimacy with Leo for fear he might detect cracks in her facade. She had grown emotionally distant, making every shared moment at home increasingly difficult to endure. She knew her silence and detachment were widening the chasm between them, but she saw no way out without risking the total destruction of everything she knew.

Her interactions with Jürgen were marked by contradictions. He continued to make her feel special, encouraging her to break free from the constraints of her domestic life while tightening the trap around her. The promises he made of a new life and regained freedom were mere illusions to keep her compliant. Every encounter with him only deepened her enslavement. Eva was living in an invisible prison, its walls built from empty promises and skillful lies.

Gradually, the line between her public and secret lives began to blur. Eva was losing herself in the role imposed by the network, losing control of her own identity. Each day was filled with lies to Leo, forced smiles masking her guilt and shame. Her life became a series of strategies for concealment, half-truths, and veiled acts of betrayal. The weight of her double life became unbearable, yet fear of exposure kept her in a state of total paralysis.

Eva knew this situation couldn't last forever. Sooner or later, the truth would come out, with devastating consequences for her, Leo, and their children. But for now, she felt she had no choice but to continue playing her role, each day becoming more ensnared in her choices and the manipulations of Jürgen and the network.

CHAPTER 3:

Emotional Detachment from Leo

As Jürgen Hauser, Agent Romeo, tightened his grip on Eva, the emotional distance between her and Leo became increasingly apparent and difficult to ignore. What had once been a relationship filled with tenderness and complicity slowly eroded under the weight of secrets, manipulation, and the conflicting emotions Eva struggled to conceal. This situation created an invisible chasm between the two, one that grew wider with each passing day.

Over time, Eva changed under the pressure of blackmail and the demands Jürgen placed on her. She no longer had the emotional energy to sustain her role as a loving wife and devoted mother. This emotional burden gnawed at her, yet she had no one to confide in. Leo, preoccupied with work, noticed the shift in their relationship but couldn't understand what was truly happening. He had no idea of Jürgen's hold over Eva, attributing her growing coldness to stress or the challenges of family responsibilities.

Eva, torn between two worlds, found herself in an agonizing dilemma. On one hand, she still loved Leo and felt guilty about the growing distance between them. On the other, she was trapped by Jürgen's psychological pressure. Each day, she felt increasingly powerless in the face of her situation. She feared that Leo might discover the truth about her affair, the compromising videos, and her enslavement to the criminal network. The more she lied and withdrew, the deeper her guilt and fear became, making her colder and more distant.

Jürgen, ever the manipulator, knew how to exploit the situation. He encouraged this emotional drift, knowing that the deterioration of Eva and Leo's relationship would serve his goals. He commanded her to distance herself from Leo, avoid moments of intimacy, and create tension in their marriage. Submissively, Eva complied, adding yet another layer of detachment to their once-warm relationship.

Arguments between Leo and Eva became more frequent. Frustrated by the lack of affection and her distant demeanor, Leo tried to communicate, but Eva, burdened by her inner turmoil, could no longer play the role of the loving wife she had been for so many years. At times, Leo felt as if his wife was physically present but emotionally absent, as though an invisible wall had been erected between them.

In these moments of tension and coldness, Leo began to doubt himself, unaware of the intricate plot unfolding behind the scenes. Eva, increasingly detached, was slipping away from him. Despite the warning signs, Leo had no way of realizing that this estrangement wasn't simply the result of time or external pressures but the calculated outcome of a vicious manipulation orchestrated by a criminal network in which Eva had become an unwilling pawn.

This progressive emotional drift didn't just harm their relationship as a couple; it began to take a toll on Leo as an individual. He felt something essential slipping away from them but had no idea why or how to fix it. In this space of confusion and pain, the criminal network continued its destructive work, aiming to weaken Leo by gradually stripping him of the support of the woman he loved most.

CHAPTER 4:

Eva, a Powerless Puppet

Eva, once a strong and independent woman, had gradually transformed into a puppet under the control of the criminal network and Jürgen Hauser, Agent Romeo. Her every move was calculated by the network, leaving her incapable of acting on her own desires. This total submission began with subtle manipulations, but over time, she descended into a spiral where every action, every decision, was dictated by fear and the constant threat of compromising videos.

The image of a loving, protective wife and mother had become nothing more than a facade behind which Eva hid. Inside, she felt trapped in an unending nightmare. She knew that one misstep could lead to the revelation of the videos and the complete destruction of her life. Yet, it wasn't just her reputation at stake. Eva was convinced that the network wouldn't hesitate to target her family if she disobeyed. This ever-present, looming threat kept her in a perpetual state of terror.

At this point, Eva saw herself as nothing more than a powerless puppet, stripped of all autonomy. Jürgen manipulated her at will, not only to control her but also to use her as a weapon against her own husband, Leo. The network had reduced her existence to one where her choices were no longer her own. Any attempts to break free were futile, as the trap around her tightened with every move. Jürgen continuously reminded her of the dire consequences of any rebellion, keeping her firmly under his control.

Eva suffered from constant psychological pain. Every day, she was forced to confront her actions, actions that, though imposed, made her feel as though she were betraying her husband and children. She watched helplessly as the relationship she once shared with Leo dissolved under the weight of lies and manipulation. Every word, every gesture toward Leo felt like an empty performance to hide the terror she endured within.

Jürgen's pressure wasn't only emotional, it was deeply psychological. He forced Eva to participate in actions that destabilized Leo, isolating him and rendering him vulnerable. Inadvertently, she played an active role in the destruction of her own household. Every kind word or affectionate gesture she extended to Leo was no longer genuine but a fabricated lie dictated by the network. Her once-true feelings were drowned in an ocean of guilt and fear.

Eva clung to the hope that one day she might break free from this control, but reality constantly pulled her back. Jürgen maintained an iron grip over her, and the network had meticulously accounted for every possible escape plan she could conceive. They had built a trap so intricate that she couldn't see a way out, a web of intimidation and fear that had reduced her to a completely powerless puppet.

Each passing day, Eva felt herself losing more of her identity. What frightened her most wasn't just the thought of Leo discovering the truth, but the realization that she was losing herself in this descent into hell. Memories of her once-normal life, filled with love and joy with her family, felt distant and unreal. Now, all that remained of Eva was a broken woman, trapped in a cruel game, incapable of breaking free from the invisible chains that bound her.

Leo, for his part, was still unaware of the full extent of the trap that had ensnared Eva. He noticed the changes, the growing distance between them, but couldn't identify the cause. Every attempt he made to communicate or reconnect with her met an invisible barrier. Eva, consumed by her own torment, couldn't respond to his efforts. She knew that any truth, any confession, would lead to her ultimate downfall.

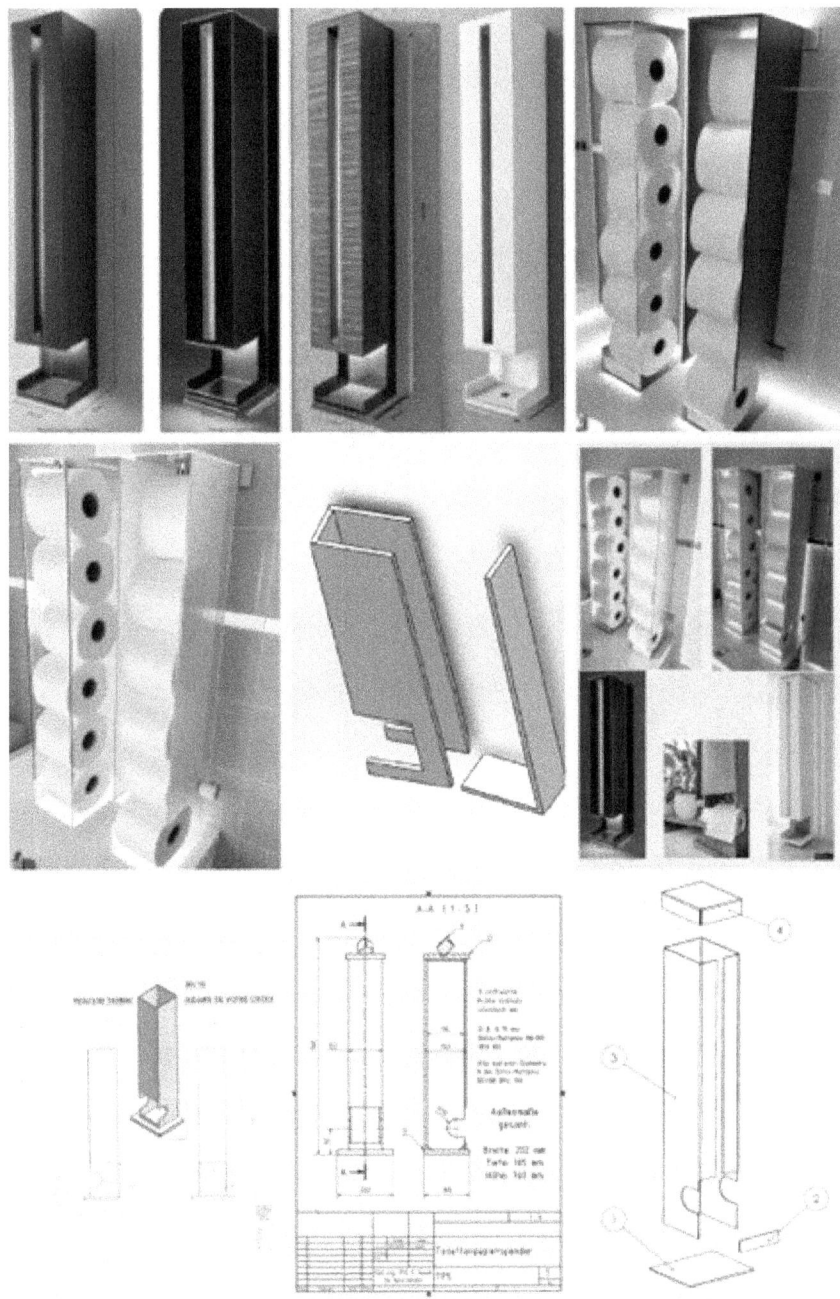

PART 4:

Eva's Mission: Driving Leo to Suicide

Chapters:

1. The Criminals' Orders: Breaking Leo Psychologically

2. Eva, the Unwilling Instrument of Destruction

3. The Mental Torture Orchestrated by Eva

4. Leo's Struggle Against Growing Depression

CHAPTER 1:

The Criminals' Orders: Breaking Leo Psychologically

The criminal network realized it needed to change its approach to destroy Leo. After the failed assassination attempts, they understood that the key to his downfall lay in psychological destruction. It was no longer about trying to kill him physically but about mentally eroding him to the point where he could no longer withstand the pressure and would self-destruct. They knew that a man like Leo, strong and resilient, couldn't be taken down with brute force. But no one is invulnerable to an attack from within, especially when orchestrated by those who are supposed to love and protect them. This is why they decided to use Eva, who was already under their control.

Clear and Ruthless Orders for Eva

The network gave Eva precise and merciless instructions: she was to break Leo by gradually undermining his confidence. This process would be insidious, gradual, and cruel. It wasn't about bold or obvious actions but about small, repeated acts, subtle comments and actions meant to push Leo into doubt and isolation. Trapped by compromising videos and the constant threats from the network, Eva had no choice but to obey.

One of the first orders given to Eva was to sabotage Leo's professional career by undermining his projects. Eva was to act subtly, altering documents, intercepting important communications, or delaying critical deadlines. Each small act contributed to Leo's efforts failing without him understanding why. Gradually, he would see his work deteriorate, and this continuous sense of failure would begin to shake his confidence in his own abilities.

Planting Doubts About His Mental Health

The network also knew that Leo drew great strength from his family relationships. They instructed Eva to undermine this foundation from within by provoking petty arguments, creating tension, and depriving him of emotional support. The cruelest tactic, however, was to make him doubt his own mental health.

Already destabilized by professional failures and inexplicable setbacks, Leo began questioning what was happening to him. Every time he expressed concern or doubt, Eva was instructed to respond condescendingly, suggesting he was being paranoid or imagining things.

She would say things like, "You're overthinking it," or "You're too stressed; you need to rest." Eva's role was to convince him, little by little, that his perceptions were distorted and that he was losing control. This psychological manipulation aimed to make him doubt himself and question his own lucidity. Eva had to act subtly, maintaining the illusion that everything was fine while driving him deeper into doubt.

Emotional Pressure and Sabotage

The third phase of the plan targeted Leo's emotional stability. Eva, following the network's orders, had to create scenes of tension and anxiety. She manipulated Leo's insecurities, made him feel guilty for things he hadn't done, and accused him of neglecting their relationship or failing as a father.

The more she emotionally distanced herself from him, the more isolated and destabilized Leo felt, unable to understand why. Sleepless nights became increasingly frequent for Leo. Eva, following the criminals' directives, began accusing him of not being good enough, of no longer being the man she married. She accused him of neglect and selfishness while playing her well-orchestrated role of pushing him to his breaking point.

Desperately searching for answers, Leo tried to re-establish dialogue, but Eva, still guided by the network, made him feel like he was the problem. She insinuated that he needed to change, seek help, and that he was responsible for everything going wrong in their lives. This isolated him further, depriving him of the emotional support he needed.

Leo's Resistance Wears Down

One of the most perverse aspects of this plan was that it unfolded in the shadows. Leo had no idea that his wife, the woman he loved and trusted implicitly, had become the primary instrument of his destruction. He sensed that something was wrong but couldn't pinpoint the source of his unease. He attributed the tension in their marriage to everyday stresses, fatigue, or responsibilities.

Unbeknownst to him, Eva was following orders to destroy him from within, constantly under the threat of compromising videos.

Meanwhile, Eva lived in perpetual agony. Though acting under duress, guilt consumed her. Every lie, every betrayal against Leo tore her apart a little more, but she had no choice but to continue, knowing that disobedience would mean her own downfall. She had become a tool of psychological destruction, unable to escape the web in which she was trapped.

The network, for its part, monitored the situation closely, waiting patiently for Leo to break, for his mental resilience to crumble, and for him to be pushed to the brink of despair.

CHAPTER 2:

Eva, the Unwilling Instrument of Destruction

Eva could never have imagined, even in her worst nightmares, that she would become the weapon used to destroy her husband, Leo. Yet, trapped by the manipulations and blackmail of the criminal network, she was now forced to act under their orders. This powerful and ruthless network had found in Eva the perfect leverage to reach Leo. They no longer sought to attack him directly but to dismantle him from within, through his own wife. This Machiavellian plan didn't require brute force but meticulous psychological deconstruction.

The First Manipulations and Eva's Dilemmas

At first, Eva thought she could contain the situation, believing that her involvement with Agent Romeo, aka Jürgen Hauser, would remain a fleeting secret, an affair without lasting consequences. But she had underestimated the network's reach and its ability to exploit emotional vulnerabilities. The moment she was ensnared by the compromising videos, Eva lost all control. Each recorded video, every betrayal captured, drove her deeper into a situation with no visible escape.

Eva was forced to live a double life. On one side, she maintained the role of a loving wife and attentive mother. On the other, she received detailed and cruel instructions from the network to sabotage Leo's life. The orders went far beyond mere lies or omissions. She had to provoke arguments, question his professional decisions, and create a constant atmosphere of tension in their home. Every conflict, every heavy silence was orchestrated by the network to emotionally destabilize Leo.

Professional and Personal Sabotage

One of the most insidious tasks assigned to Eva was to subtly sabotage Leo's work. It wasn't blatant sabotage but small, repeated actions that would quietly undermine his success. Eva was instructed to delay appointments, hide important documents, and introduce errors into his professional files, all under the guise of ignorance or apparent clumsiness.

These seemingly minor acts began to harm Leo. His projects faced delays, professional opportunities evaporated, and he couldn't understand why his once-thriving career was slowly unraveling.

Doubt Creeps In for Leo

Initially confident in himself, Leo began to doubt. The once-solid man, at the peak of a brilliant career, suddenly faced a string of inexplicable failures. Unbeknownst to him, his wife, acting under duress, had become a pawn of the criminal network, sabotaging his efforts at every turn.

Eva, meanwhile, endured a constant inner torment. Each action against Leo destroyed her a little more, yet she was bound hand and foot. She knew that defying Jürgen's orders would lead to everything being exposed, and she would lose far more than her marriage.

An Unwilling Instrument

What tore Eva apart the most was realizing that she played a direct role in her husband's downfall. Her actions, though unwilling, contributed to Leo's destruction, little by little, every day. But she couldn't bring herself to tell him the truth or warn him of the danger. Every word, every action was controlled by the network, forcing her to continue this destructive role, even as it consumed her from within.

She watched Leo's distress grow, his frustration, his mental exhaustion, but she couldn't do anything to help him. On the contrary, she was compelled to fuel these feelings, to intensify the mental destabilization the network sought. Eva had become the instrument of his psychological destruction, a role she would never have chosen but felt condemned to play. She was a puppet, fully aware of the harm she was causing yet powerless to stop the infernal cycle.

The Fatal Spiral

Eva found herself caught in a spiral she couldn't escape. The deeper she went into the criminals' plan, the more she realized she could never turn back. Her life and Leo's were disintegrating before her eyes, and she was the central figure in this tragedy, though against her will. The criminal network had orchestrated an implacable scheme, and Eva was now the unwilling instrument of the destruction of the man she loved, an act that would scar her forever.

Leo, for his part, was still trying to understand what was happening. He could sense that something had changed, that his relationship with Eva was no longer the same, but he couldn't imagine the scale of the betrayal. His suspicions were vague, lost amid the confusion of his professional failures and the growing distance between him and his wife. The network, invisible but omnipresent, continued to use Eva to achieve its ultimate goal: breaking Leo from the inside.

CHAPTER 3:

The Mental Torture Orchestrated by Eva

The manipulation of Eva reached unbearable heights when she was ordered to push Leo to the brink of psychological collapse. The criminals, after failing to eliminate him physically, opted for a more insidious approach: to destroy Leo from within, breaking him mentally until he could no longer cope. Eva, now an unwilling pawn in their plan, found herself forced to mentally torture the man she had once loved.

Following Jürgen Hauser's Orders: Gradual Isolation

Under the directives of Agent Romeo, Jürgen Hauser, Eva was instructed to gradually isolate Leo and make him doubt himself and his reality. The initial instructions seemed almost trivial: she was to provoke small arguments over insignificant matters, introduce constant disagreements about minor daily decisions. These repeated quarrels slowly eroded Leo's emotional stability, plunging him into a constant state of confusion. Once a confident and self-assured man, Leo began questioning his decisions, his judgment, and, most devastatingly, his own mental health.

Disturbing Behaviors: Daily Manipulations

The network didn't stop at subtle actions. Over time, they intensified their control over Eva, demanding increasingly bizarre and destabilizing behaviors. Against her will, Eva adopted unsettling attitudes to further disrupt Leo. For instance, she would stare at the ceiling while pointing, pretending to see something invisible. When Leo asked what she was looking at, she would respond with disdain, saying, "You're crazy. What are you talking about?"

To worsen the situation, she made cruel remarks, suggesting he should pray often because he seemed to be losing his sanity. She even insinuated that his days were numbered due to his alleged madness. These comments weren't just meant to hurt Leo, they aimed to plant deeper seeds of doubt in his mind, pulling him further away from reality and into a spiral of uncertainty. Despite having survived previous assassination attempts, Leo found himself vulnerable to these psychological attacks coming from within his own home.

Invalidating Reality and Financial Manipulation

One of the most cruel tactics involved financial sabotage. Eva began using Leo's credit cards without his authorization, withdrawing significant sums of money. When confronted, she vehemently denied any involvement, making Leo believe he was losing control entirely. This was particularly difficult for Leo to process, as they had only young children, and the credit cards had never been stolen. He was left facing an unsolvable mystery, further cementing his belief that he was losing touch with reality.

Under the criminal network's influence, Eva also stopped performing some household responsibilities. For example, she stopped cooking meals for their children. What had once been a clear division of household duties, Eva preparing family meals, vanished without explanation. Leo and the children were left eating canned food, a deliberate strategy to destabilize Leo by disrupting the constants of his daily life, including Eva's traditional role.

Emotional and Physical Poisoning

The only seemingly affectionate act Eva maintained was preparing coffee for Leo. However, even this was a disguised betrayal. Leo eventually realized, far too late, that the coffee was poisoned. While the poison acted subtly, it progressively weakened his body, leaving him increasingly vulnerable and exhausted. Leo lost nearly 30 kilograms, unable to eat properly. At times, he went three days without food, surviving only on the coffee that was destroying him from the inside.

The physical toll became so visible that when a longtime family friend saw him in public, she burst into tears at the sight of how frail he had become. His pants, too loose to stay up, had to be held in place by hand to avoid falling.

Intimacy and Emotional Isolation

On an intimate level, Eva's torture took another turn. She refused any sexual relations, claiming to be tired or disinterested. Yet at night, she would masturbate beside Leo in their marital bed, amplifying his feelings of rejection and confusion. When she did agree to sexual relations, it was with cold detachment, asking him to hurry as she was "too tired" to prolong the act. This cruel treatment, both physical and emotional, chipped away at Leo's mental health, leaving him struggling to make sense of the contradictory behaviors.

Family and Social Isolation

The network's plan extended beyond Leo's home, seeking to isolate him from his family and friends. Eva began spreading lies about Leo's mental health to his siblings, claiming he was losing his mind and urging them to take him away before it was too late. She also intercepted important phone calls from his family, even going as far as unplugging the home phone's cable. These actions aimed to sever Leo's external support systems, plunging him further into solitude.

Entrapped in a Destructive Spiral

Desperate and cornered, Leo felt his world crumbling. Every gesture and word from Eva reinforced the image of a man losing his sanity. The cruel truth, however, was that it wasn't Leo who was losing his mind, it was Eva who, under the criminal network's pressure, had become the instrument of his mental torture.

As Leo desperately tried to understand what was happening, the destructive spiral orchestrated by the network continued to drag him further into darkness.

Eva's mental torture of Leo had reached a point of no return. Physically and emotionally exhausted, Leo was teetering on the edge. And yet, he remained oblivious to the true plot against him, a conspiracy in which the woman he loved had become the cornerstone, albeit against her will.

CHAPTER 4:

Leo's Struggle Against Growing Depression

Slowly but surely, Leo sank into a deep depression. The weight of the manipulations orchestrated by the criminal network, Eva's distant attitude, and the sabotage of his daily life created an emotional storm he could no longer ignore. His nights were restless, haunted by dark thoughts and recurring nightmares. Days seemed to stretch endlessly, each moment reminding him that he was trapped in a reality he could no longer control.

The first signs of his depression were subtle but persistent: unexplained fatigue, increasing difficulty in completing daily tasks, and a gradual loss of interest in the things that had once brought him joy. Leo, who had once been energetic and dynamic, now felt drained of all vitality. He struggled to get out of bed in the morning, and even managing his business, which had always been a source of pride, seemed insurmountable. Every interaction with colleagues or loved ones required a considerable effort, leaving him feeling increasingly isolated in his suffering.

During this period, Eva worked to make the situation even more unbearable. Following the network's instructions, she accused Leo of being responsible for all the problems in their relationship. She called him a bad father, emphasizing that he spent more time focused on work than on caring for his family. She called him "mentally ill" and "schizophrenic," words that, through repetition, began to sow doubt in Leo's mind. These accusations, repeated day after day, weakened him and fed his growing guilt.

Eva didn't stop there. She worked to isolate Leo not only from his children but also from his friends and family. By telling the children that Leo was "mean," she further eroded the family bonds. With his friends and relatives, she created distance by spreading lies and slander, widening the gap between Leo and those who might have supported him. Several times, she intercepted phone calls from his loved ones, even going so far as to deliberately unplug the home phone cable. This deliberate manipulation plunged Leo into overwhelming solitude, cutting him off from the exchanges and external support he so desperately needed.

The worst part came with the introduction of alcohol into their lives. Eva, following the network's plan, began purchasing strong alcoholic drinks and encouraging Leo to drink with her. Hoping it might ease their relationship or at least provide a brief respite, Leo agreed. What he didn't know was that Eva was pretending to drink, secretly pouring her own drinks into a plant at every opportunity. When Leo was sufficiently drunk, she added a mysterious liquid to his drinks, similar to what she had used in his coffee, which multiplied the effects of the alcohol and weakened him even more.

When he was in this state, she took advantage of his vulnerability to whisper destructive words: "A real man would have already ended his life. You're a disgrace, a dishonor." This phrase echoed in his mind repeatedly, planting an insidious idea: that the only way out of his torment would be to throw himself out of the sixth-floor window, as she repeatedly suggested. Every day, Eva increased the mental pressure, and Leo's isolation, combined with the growing distance from his children, weighed more heavily on him.

Leo, for his part, tried to cling to reality, but he could sense that something was wrong. Recent events, Eva's behavior, everything seemed like pieces of a puzzle he couldn't fully understand. He found himself trapped in a vicious cycle of confusion, mental exhaustion, and doubt. He no longer knew whom to trust, or even if his perceptions were still reliable. His physical health deteriorated, his body wasting away, and his mind plunged deeper into the darkness of depression.

In the midst of this emotional storm, Leo was left alone, lost, and terrified. He tried to understand what was happening to him, but every time he approached an explanation, reality slipped further away. The noose tightened, and he wondered how much longer he could hold on before succumbing to the crushing pressure of the manipulations orchestrated against him.

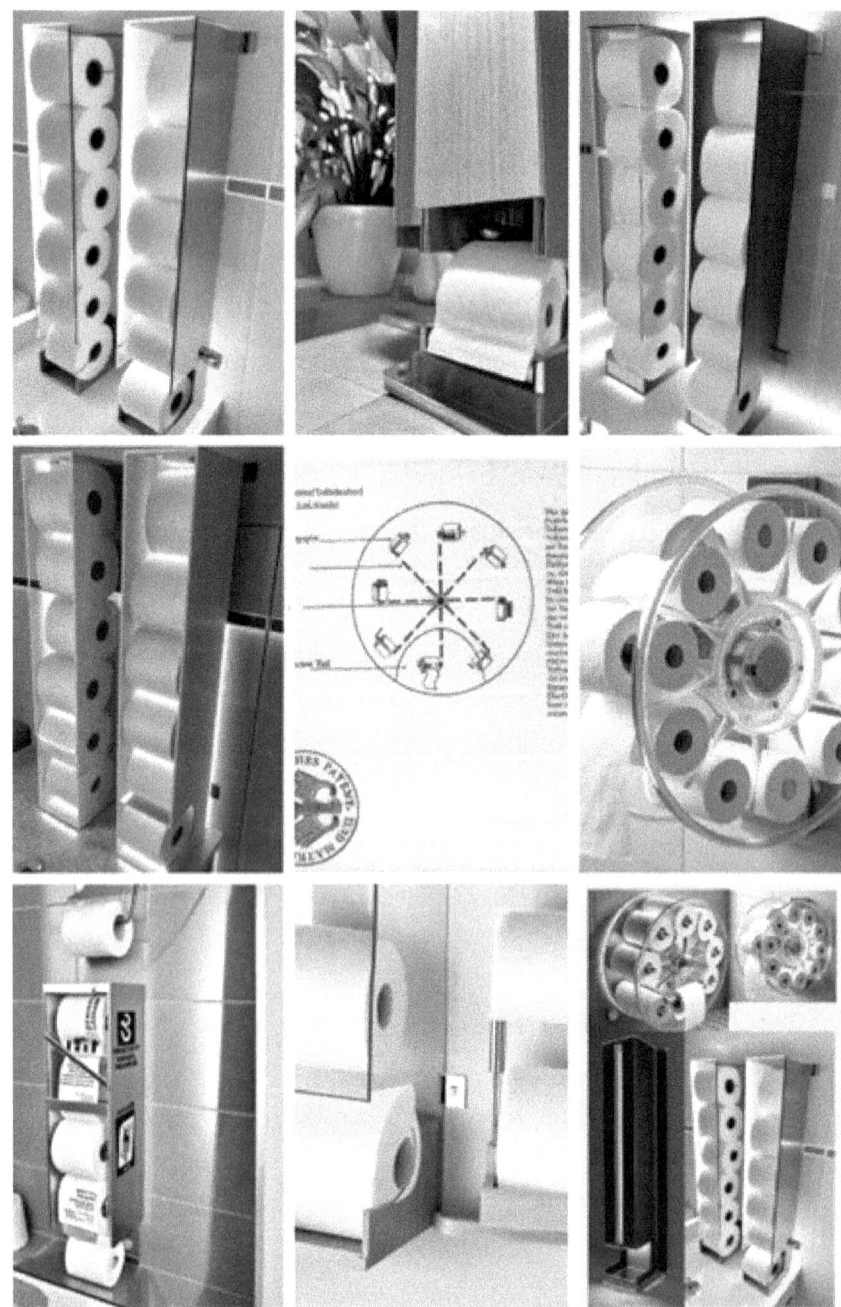

PART 5:

Making Leo Appear Insane

Chapters:

1. A New, More Insidious Strategy

2. Gradual Discrediting

3. Subtle Psychological Manipulations

4. Leo Begins to Doubt His Mental Health

CHAPTER 1:

A New, More Insidious Strategy

Leander P. had an obsession with cryptic expressions. "The fish always rots from the head," he liked to repeat with a sly smile, as if holding a secret no one else could grasp. And then there was his reference to Hansel and Gretel, whispered during late-night strategy sessions, a sinister murmur that transformed the innocent story into a chilling metaphor. Leo and Eva were the lost children wandering through a dark forest, while they, the network, were the witch, ready to consume them slowly.

After failing to neutralize Leo through direct means, the network resolved to destroy him mentally, a subtle downfall orchestrated with diabolical precision. If Leo was the head of the fish, then their strategy was to poison him from within until he completely disintegrated. Eva, his wife, became the central piece of this insidious destruction.

Everything depended on slowness and subtlety: to reduce Leo to a wreck, one small dose at a time. For this, Leander P. endlessly repeated his metaphor: "The fish always rots from the head." The network didn't need a frontal assault; a constant erosion would suffice. Every detail of the plan was meticulously designed to strike Leo at his most vulnerable points: his home, his loved ones, his values.

Leander P. also loved referencing Hansel and Gretel as a perfect allegory. "The lost children," he would say with a fierce grin. Leo and Eva were those children venturing into a dark forest filled with trials. But unlike the fairy tale, there was no promise of rescue at the end. Their "witch" was the network, an invisible but omnipresent force manipulating every aspect of their lives.

The goal wasn't just to destroy Leo but to witness his collapse. This downfall had to be slow and public, so that his support system, his colleagues, his family, could watch him deteriorate, powerless to help. The weapon of choice for this assault wasn't physical but Eva herself, transformed into the catalyst for orchestrated chaos.

"This won't be brutal, but it will be magnificent," declared Jürgen Hauser, nicknamed "Agent Romeo." His role was clear:

to win over Eva, not with love, but through psychological domination. It wasn't enough to distance her from Leo; he had to reshape her, destabilizing her mental state and stripping her of any moral or emotional bearings. "Hansel and Gretel had no one to show them the way," he sometimes whispered to Eva, planting the idea that she was alone and had to survive at any cost.

The network had been patient. The first signs of tension were subtly sown: small insinuations in Eva's conversations with Leo, seemingly insignificant decisions with heavy consequences. Then came the gradual isolation: Eva stopped talking to her close friends, choosing instead to confide in Jürgen. Leo noticed the changes late, absences he attributed to stress, moments of coldness he tried to thaw with outdated gestures of affection.

"The fish always rots from the head, but it's the guts that betray it first," Leander P. liked to say with his signature dark relish. The goal was to destabilize Leo on every front: as a husband, a father, and a professional. His certainties were their target. Every element of the plan had to be unpredictable yet inevitable.

And yet, there was a perverse beauty in their approach. Nothing was left to chance: every phrase, every event, every calculated glance was designed to maximize confusion. Leo, a rational man, found his rationality turning into his enemy in the face of these carefully measured manipulations.

Leander P. described this strategy in his notes as a "soft implosion." No direct violence. No frontal confrontation. Just a systematic, inevitable collapse until Leo lost trust in everything that defined him.

Hansel and Gretel also served as a metaphor for the double game. Eva was both victim and perpetrator, unknowingly. She was the bait but also the instrument of continuous misinformation. At every stage, Jürgen ensured she felt guilty but never enough to break her connection to Leo. This was part of their art: maintaining a precarious balance between hope and destruction.

And at the top of this scaffolding of lies stood Leander P. For him, this wasn't just an operation, it was a demonstration of power, a perverse game he conducted with the precision of a symphony conductor. He observed every move, every interaction between Leo and Eva, savoring the results. With each step forward, he murmured, "The fish always rots from the head. And they don't even see themselves falling apart."

CHAPTER 2:

Gradual Discrediting

The criminal network, led by Jürgen and his accomplices, entered a new phase of their plan, aiming to discredit Leo in a subtle yet relentless manner. Aware that physical or direct attacks would not suffice to break him, they decided to employ psychological methods focused on social isolation and gradual discrediting. Their objective: to slowly undermine Leo's reputation in the eyes of his loved ones, colleagues, and family while depriving him of the moral support that could have protected him.

Eva, completely under Jürgen's control, became the perfect tool to execute this plan. The power dynamic between Eva and Jürgen was clear: she was nothing more than a puppet, blindly obeying his orders. Jürgen had gradually brought her to a state of submission where she had no choice but to comply with his demands, despite the consequences for her own life and Leo's.

Their relationship was not merely that of a manipulator and victim but that of a master and his slave. Jürgen had pushed this dynamic to the point where he even handed her over to other people to fulfill their fantasies, plunging her into constant humiliation.

The process of discrediting Leo was methodical. Eva started with seemingly innocent but repeated remarks to mutual friends and family. She suggested that Leo had changed, that he was becoming strange, less stable, and no longer the man he used to be. These insinuations, delivered softly and subtly, began to sow doubt among those who heard them. Eva, under Jürgen's orders, knew how to measure these remarks so that the listeners wouldn't suspect manipulation. Phrases like, "He barely sleeps these days," or "I'm worried about him; he seems so nervous," were enough to instill latent concern.

This strategy worked particularly well because Leo, already weakened by previous psychological attacks and tension with Eva, began to show real signs of fatigue and stress. Eva's remarks resonated with their audience, reinforcing the image of a man on the verge of collapse. The criminal network, always in the background, monitored the impact of these words. They knew that with each new suggestion from Eva, Leo's reputation deteriorated further.

Eva's manipulation wasn't limited to private circles. She also played a role in tarnishing Leo's professional reputation. Following Jürgen's advice, she planted doubts in the minds of Leo's colleagues, suggesting that he was becoming unstable and irrational. She insinuated that he was irritable at work, made poor decisions, and might need psychological help. Over time, these insinuations found traction, and some colleagues began doubting Leo's ability to lead his business.

But the most pernicious part of the plan was isolating Leo from his family. Eva used sneaky tactics to cut Leo off from his loved ones. For example, she frequently unplugged the house phone, preventing Leo from receiving calls from family members. During family gatherings or conversations with his siblings, Eva insinuated that Leo had become unpredictable or was "voluntarily isolating himself." This strategy, combined with the other schemes, gradually damaged Leo's relationships with his family. They began believing he was experiencing a deep crisis, further increasing his isolation.

At the same time, Eva became more aggressive in manipulating Leo directly. She repeatedly told him that he was "no longer the same," that he needed to "see a professional," or that he was "exaggerating" by seeing enemies where there were none. This form of psychological manipulation, known as gaslighting, gradually made Leo doubt his own reality. He started to believe that his concerns were imaginary and that he might indeed be becoming paranoid.

The process of gradual discrediting was executed with ruthless precision. As Leo found himself isolated from his family and friends, he began losing his footing. Each remark from Eva, each insinuation about his mental health, widened the gap between him and those who might have supported him. Even his closest colleagues started questioning his ability to lead, further contributing to his total isolation. Jürgen and the network had successfully created an environment where Leo was completely vulnerable, without allies or resources to defend himself.

Thus, this strategy of gradual discrediting was not aimed at attacking Leo directly but at eroding him from within, using the people he trusted most. Trapped in this web of lies and manipulation, Leo found himself alone, unable to understand why everything around him was falling apart. Eva, completely under Jürgen's control, played her role decisively, contributing every day to her husband's downfall while sinking deeper into a pit she could never escape.

Eva, pushed by Jürgen to sow suspicion, adopted an even more insidious approach to discredit Leo. In casual conversations with loved ones, she suggested that her husband might be involved in mysterious or even dubious activities. It was a subtle poison, delivered with carefully chosen words and a concerned but calculated tone. She hinted to others that Leo always had a "dark side," something he had hidden, even after all the years they'd spent together.

Example of manipulation:

During a meeting with a close couple of friends, Eva chose her words carefully: "You know, lately, Leo has been so... different. I've never really known what he does during the day. I'm starting to wonder if he's hiding something, something I've never known about." This subtle insinuation acted as a silent bomb. The friends, though surprised, began to question him. After all, if his own wife doubted him, surely there must be a reason?

Gradually, Eva accelerated her insidious narrative, portraying Leo as a man capable of unspeakable secrets. She hinted he might even be associated with a suspicious group of people she didn't know but believed had changed him. She planted doubts by claiming to have found enigmatic documents or emails among Leo's belongings, further fueling her supposed concerns.

Eva's thoughts:

"How could I have lived with him all this time without knowing who he really was? Maybe I've been blind... Maybe he's always had this hidden side, and I just refused to see it." These thoughts, largely fabricated by Jürgen and the network, deeply rooted themselves in Eva's mind, becoming almost a truth to her.

Leo's psychological tension:

On his side, Leo noticed that people around him were beginning to act differently. He perceived avoiding gazes, forced smiles, and unusual silences in conversations that were once warm and sincere. His friends and colleagues, influenced by Eva's insinuations, were slowly distancing themselves. Leo felt this growing isolation but couldn't understand why he was suddenly being viewed with suspicion. This incomprehension plunged him further into confusion and doubt.

Eva went so far as to hint that Leo might be dishonest. She confided to her close circle that she was discovering "things" about him she'd never thought possible. She insinuated that he might have financial secrets, hidden debts, or even bank accounts she didn't know about.

This campaign of discredit began dismantling the foundations of Leo's reputation, a cornerstone of his identity. Each insinuation, each suspicious glance, eroded his confidence and deepened his sense of isolation. The atmosphere of suspicion created by Eva formed a bubble of anxiety and paranoia around Leo. Without knowing it, Leo became a pawn in a far more complex scheme than he could imagine, where the face of his enemy was that of his own wife.

CHAPTER 3:

Subtle Psychological Manipulations

The war waged by the criminal network against Leo had transformed into an invisible but intense psychological battle, designed to shake his emotional and mental foundations. To achieve this, Jürgen and the network understood that direct attacks would not be enough to destabilize this resilient man. Their strategy now focused on a slow and insidious erosion of his perception of reality, orchestrated by Eva herself, under Jürgen's firm control.

At first, Eva's manipulations were subtle, almost innocuous. She would deliberately misplace Leo's important belongings, his keys, wallet, or essential work documents, moving them to different locations without his knowledge. These small disruptions in his daily routine sowed confusion. Whenever he asked her if she had seen the missing item, she would respond with calculated indifference, assuring him she hadn't touched anything. This "gaslighting" began to affect Leo's perception, trapping him in a dilemma: had he really lost these items, or was his mind playing tricks on him?

Gradually, Eva began altering their shared memories as well. When they discussed past events, she recounted distorted versions of what had happened, denying details Leo knew to be accurate. She might describe an innocuous situation while claiming Leo had overreacted or had forgotten an essential part of the event. Her deliberate insistence started to weaken Leo, making him question whether his own memories were reliable. This growing sense of confusion and doubt settled within him, like a thick fog clouding his ability to discern reality.

Eva's attacks weren't limited to memory and object manipulation; they took on a cruel emotional dimension as well. She constantly criticized him, attacking his personality and his role as a father. "You're never there for the kids. You don't care about us anymore, Leo. It's like you don't love your family." Each remark cut deeply, forcing Leo into painful self-reflection. He tried to win back her love and trust, but every effort was met with cold criticism or silent rejection. This cycle of hope and rejection amplified his suffering, leaving him with a constant sense of failure.

Isolating Leo also became a priority for the network, and Eva, under Jürgen's control, worked methodically to sever his social connections. She found excuses to prevent visits from relatives, sometimes unplugged the phone to block incoming calls, and sowed doubt among his colleagues and friends. During the rare interactions he had with loved ones, Eva played the role of the concerned wife, emphasizing that Leo was behaving strangely. To his friends, she dropped lines like: "He spends less and less time with us; he's getting more and more nervous." These subtle insinuations planted seeds of doubt among his circle, who, over time, began to distrust Leo as well.

The cumulative effect of these manipulations was devastating. Leo felt trapped in a spiral of isolation and doubt. Even in rare moments of apparent calm, Eva maintained a constant psychological pressure. Sometimes, in an unsettling quiet, she would say to him: "You should pray, Leo. There's something dark inside you, and it might be your end." Every word, every action seemed to reinforce the idea that Leo was losing his grip, that his mind was unraveling.

Jürgen's strategy, though subtle, aimed to undermine Leo from within. By using Eva as an instrument of psychological destruction, he created an invisible cage around Leo, with every doubt and suspicion serving as additional bars. Leo, already weakened by loneliness and a lack of support, saw his confidence in himself and his perception of reality erode inexorably, bringing him closer to the brink with each passing day.

CHAPTER 4:

Leo Begins to Doubt His Mental Health

The impact of Eva's manipulations on Leo's mind was reaching its peak. For months, he had been subjected to relentless psychological pressure. What had begun as small anomalies and isolated incidents had morphed into a living nightmare, a hell where each day seemed darker and more surreal than the last. Now, even the simplest realities of his daily life appeared to crumble. This incessant doubt and disorientation affected every aspect of his existence, gnawing away at his rational mind and his ability to trust his own perceptions.

Leo, once a stable and balanced man, now viewed even the most basic interactions through a lens of confusion and distrust. The environment Eva had crafted for him resembled a labyrinth of manipulations, where every word, every behavior, planted more seeds of doubt. She ensnared him with bewildering accusations, questioning his memory and perceptions, making him believe he was losing his mind. When he tried to discuss his concerns with her, she would meet him with a chilling calmness and respond in a neutral voice, "Leo, you're losing it. You're imagining things."

This subtle manipulation strategy, known as gaslighting, amplified his sense of despair. Leo found himself in a constant state of mental confusion. He no longer knew where to find solace or whom to confide in. His loved ones, influenced by Eva's false concerns, began looking at him differently, avoiding his calls, and silently questioning his mental stability. The progressive isolation Eva orchestrated so skillfully left Leo vulnerable, depriving him of the support he might have found in his family and friends.

Leo tried to hold on to some clarity, but the constant pressure drove him to doubt his own sanity more and more. Eva's repeated manipulations, misplaced objects, altered memories, and implicit accusations, became a form of psychological torture. Her words echoed obsessively in his mind, leaving an invisible but deeply etched mark on his psyche. At every moment, he questioned whether he was truly descending into madness.

As the days passed, Leo felt increasingly disconnected from reality. He began observing his own behavior, searching for signs of the "illness" Eva claimed he had, wondering if his actions were truly his own or the result of a deteriorating mind. This constant self-surveillance, coupled with the doubts that ate away at him, plunged Leo into growing anxiety. He began doubting even his smallest actions, his own thoughts, and his judgment.

Eva's words took a darker and more direct tone over time. She no longer hesitated to suggest that, in her view, he wouldn't be able to lead a normal life much longer. "You're sick, Leo. I can see it in your eyes… you don't have much time left." These phrases, whispered under her breath, left Leo in a state of intense panic. The idea that his mental health was deteriorating became a daily torment, an obsession that consumed his every waking moment.

The criminal network's strategy was bearing fruit. The strong and rational Leo, who had always kept a cool head in the face of adversity, now stood at the edge of a mental abyss. He clung to the hope that this disintegration of his reality was just a phase, a difficult period he could overcome. But each new insinuation from Eva, each pitying or suspicious look from his loved ones, dragged him deeper into a spiral of doubt.

In his despair, Leo found himself trapped in an unbearable inner conflict: Was he truly going insane, or was he the victim of a conspiracy so masterfully constructed that he couldn't prove it to anyone, not even himself? This question, haunting him day and night, was the culmination of the criminal network's plan: to break Leo without a single direct blow, forcing him to self-destruct from within, driven by a falsified reality and a love betrayed.

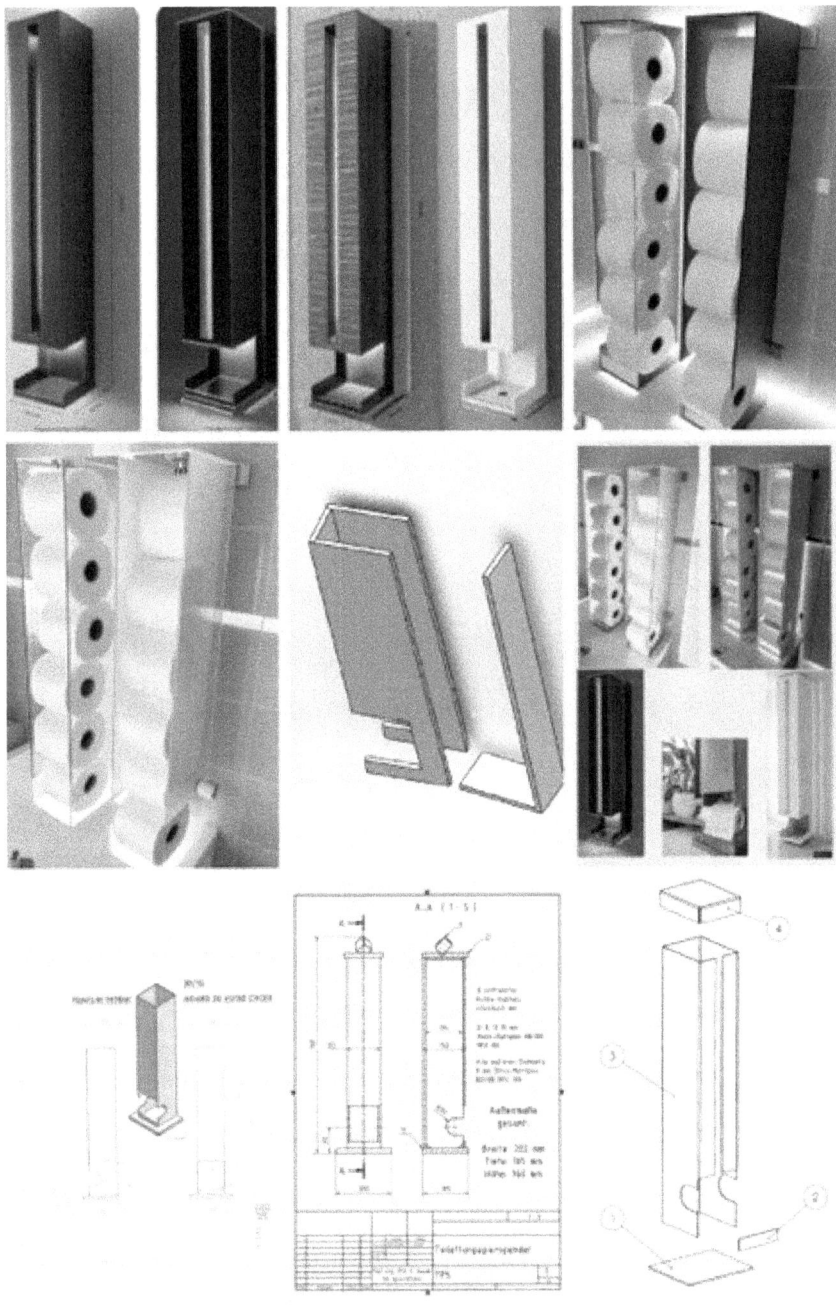

PART 6:

The Shadows Deepen

Chapters:

1. Leo senses a change, without understanding it
2. Eva becomes more distant and absent
3. Leo fails to notice the signs of manipulation
4. The criminal network tightens its grip

CHAPTER 1:

Leo senses a change, without understanding it

Leo had a vague sense that something had radically changed in his life, but he couldn't pinpoint exactly what. Every day, he noticed troubling details, tiny signs that seemed to pile up, surrounding him with an oppressive and bewildering atmosphere. This diffuse sense of unease, gripping him relentlessly, felt like a thick fog clouding his mind.

Eva's behavior, first and foremost, had become an enigma. Leo remembered the loving and attentive woman she had always been, but that closeness seemed to have vanished. He tried to reconnect with her, to spark moments of tenderness, but he was met with a coldness that chilled his heart. Eva, who had once shared in the small joys of daily life, had grown increasingly distant, almost mechanical in her interactions. She seemed absent even when she was there, as if she was hiding something behind her gaze.

Every attempt at communication with her bogged down in misunderstandings. When Leo expressed his concerns, Eva turned the tables, insinuating that he was becoming paranoid, gradually trapping him in his own doubts. Her subtle, disconcerting remarks planted seeds of confusion in his mind. One day, he caught Eva murmuring while staring at an invisible point on the ceiling. When he asked her what she was looking at, she gave him a cold look, as if he made no sense, and murmured, "You're crazy, Leo." These words seeped into his mind, plunging him into deep worry.

The signs of this change also piled up in the details of daily life. Leo noticed objects being moved without explanation, documents he thought he had filed away mysteriously disappearing. Sometimes, he found notes written in his handwriting in unexpected places, leaving him with the feeling that someone was playing games with him. These moments of confusion felt like cracks in his reality, breaches where logic slipped away.

His relationship with his children was also deteriorating, subtly but poignantly. Eva seemed to position herself between them, planting doubts about him in their minds. Leo often found himself alone with his feelings as a father, unable to understand why his children, who once confided in him naturally, now seemed wary, even cold. This distance, orchestrated in the shadows, weakened him in his role as a father, and every look of mistrust he saw in his children's eyes chipped away at him a little more.

At home, even ordinary objects seemed cloaked in silence, as though they were watching, inanimate witnesses to the slow dissolution of his family life. Family photos disappeared from the walls, and photo albums were suddenly stowed away in unusual places. The house, once a haven of peace, seemed permeated with an invisible but constant discomfort, a weight pressing down on Leo's shoulders at every moment.

He tried to reassure himself that all of this was temporary, but the accumulation of Eva's troubling behavior and the strange events around him began to undermine his perception. He wondered if he was, in fact, being overly suspicious, creating problems where there were none. Yet every attempt at rationalization collapsed as soon as a new incident occurred: a strange look from Eva, an insidious comment, a lack of response where once she would have been kind.

Leo began to doubt his own mental health, torn between a deep intuition that something terrible was unfolding and the haze of uncertainty that Eva's manipulations had instilled in his mind. For the first time in his life, he felt like a prisoner in his own home, trapped in the toxic atmosphere that was gradually enveloping him.

CHAPTER 2:

Eva becomes more distant and absent

As the criminal network's trap closed tighter around her, Eva became a shadow, a barely present figure in Leo's life. What had begun as innocuous excuses to justify her absences had turned into a profound, almost irreversible distancing. Leo watched helplessly as this transformation unfolded, devastating him. Before him stood a stranger, someone who bore the face of the woman he had loved but whose gaze was now shrouded in an icy distance.

Each day, Eva faded a little more, seeking refuge in mysterious "outings" and endless errands that kept her away from home for hours. With every return, Leo hoped for a return to normalcy, but she seemed even more detached, as if every moment spent away from him drew her further from their shared life. Her eyes avoided his, her words were measured and often devoid of emotion, leaving Leo with the cruel feeling of being a mere spectator in his own life.

Desperately, Leo tried to understand what was wrong. He made repeated efforts to rekindle their connection, organizing family outings and suggesting romantic evenings, but his attempts were consistently rebuffed by Eva. She claimed overwork or vague discomfort, leaving Leo bewildered and frustrated. Each refusal was another wound, another sign that their relationship was slipping irreversibly toward a breaking point.

This distance was not just physical but profoundly emotional. Gestures of affection grew rare, and any attempt at intimacy was rejected with excuses of fatigue or a lack of desire. Once confident in their love, Leo now found himself consumed by uncertainty and doubt. His attempts to maintain honest communication invariably failed, as Eva deflected his questions, sometimes even turning the situation around to accuse him of being too preoccupied with his own problems.

Eva's transformation extended beyond her relationship with Leo. She also withdrew from their children, abandoning her role as a loving and attentive mother to retreat into crushing solitude. She spent hours absorbed in reading or watching television, refusing the family moments that had once brought warmth to their home. Leo, seeing his children perplexed by her absence, tried to compensate but felt he could never fill the immense void Eva left behind.

This gradual withdrawal stemmed from the overwhelming pressure exerted by the criminal network, led by Jürgen. Trapped, threatened, and subjected to repeated humiliations, Eva was no longer herself, torn between shame, guilt, and the grip of a man who controlled her to the very depths of her mind. Her distance from Leo was not a choice but a means of surviving the unbearable reality that crushed her more each day.

Deep down, Leo sensed that something more profound was at play, but he clung to the hope that the bond they shared could be restored. Yet, each passing day widened the chasm between them, eroding the foundations of their life together and leaving Leo to face an abyss of loneliness and uncertainty.

CHAPTER 3:

Leo fails to notice the signs of manipulation

Despite his analytical mind, Leo could not clearly see the signs of manipulation unfolding in his own home. The growing distance between him and Eva deeply troubled him, but he failed to recognize it as part of an insidious orchestration meant to destabilize him. Day by day, this unease grew within him, taking the form of a constant feeling of loss, as if an invisible bond was slowly unraveling, slipping out of his grasp.

Eva, once close and affectionate, seemed to drift away in a manner that was both subtle and gradual. Leo noticed it, but in his search for a rational explanation, he convinced himself that it could simply be a normal phase of marital tension, a difficult period every couple experiences. He attributed the distance to possible overwork, external concerns, or a personal crisis. He never imagined that this coldness concealed a skillful manipulation orchestrated by external forces.

In their exchanges, which had once been so sincere, a new dynamic had emerged, one filled with unspoken words and heavy silences. Eva, instead of responding to Leo's attempts to rekindle their bond, seemed to play a role, adopting a posture that alternated between accusatory and distant. When he tried to get closer to her, Eva paradoxically accused him of not being attentive enough. Disconcerted, Leo began doubting himself. Was he the one misinterpreting things? Was he losing his grip without even realizing it?

Each failure to reconnect with Eva weighed on him more heavily, reinforcing his sense of losing control in his own life. He no longer knew how to react to a wife he no longer recognized, yet he continued searching for rational explanations, unable to imagine that she could be manipulated for destructive purposes.

Despite his confusion, however, Leo sensed a dissonance, something intangible yet constant, like a faint warning. Every attempt at communication seemed to hit an invisible wall, and every evasive glance from Eva heightened a sense of unease he couldn't shake. This growing doubt within him was a sign of success for the network, which had skillfully orchestrated this gradual manipulation to make him doubt himself.

Leo was still unaware that this gap between them, this subtle yet relentless distance, was part of a much larger plan. This psychological warfare, waged under the guise of an outwardly normal marriage, plunged Leo into a spiral of questions, leaving him unsure of who or what to believe.

CHAPTER 4:

The criminal network tightens its grip

Leo, already vulnerable and engulfed in a thick fog of doubt, was now subjected to an intensified assault by the criminal network. For them, it was not just about isolating him emotionally from his family but also cutting him off from all other pillars of his life. To achieve their ultimate goal of total destruction, they tightened the noose, pushing Leo to feel completely bereft of any support.

The strategy was orchestrated by powerful and invisible figures, with every action designed as part of a larger, intricate scheme. Jürgen, the Agent Roméo, continued manipulating Eva, drawing her deeper into the gears of their operation. She, once Leo's partner and source of support, had become nothing more than a pawn, forced to play a role that was slowly destroying her from within. The network had understood well that a direct attack on Leo would be ineffective, but by using Eva, they could strike him where it hurt the most: his family life, his sanctuary.

To further tighten their grip, the network also infiltrated his professional sphere. Trusted individuals, even colleagues, received veiled instructions, masking their true intentions behind seemingly innocent actions. Important contracts, which once represented stability for Leo, were suddenly in jeopardy. Agreements he believed to be secure unraveled under improbable pretenses. Already exhausted by personal tensions, Leo no longer had the strength to understand or respond to these subtle betrayals. Each of these breaches in trust deepened his loneliness and vulnerability.

The network's tactics extended into Leo's private space. He began noticing personal items disappearing, only to reappear in unlikely places. His car keys, professional files, and even valuable possessions seemed to be moved as if an invisible hand were intruding into his life. These isolated incidents, seemingly trivial, were calculated to push him into a quiet paranoia. Over time, Leo began doubting his own perception of reality. These actions were integral to the overarching strategy, aimed at plunging him into a state of total confusion.

As for Eva, she too became a crucial instrument in the pressure exerted on Leo. The guilt she carried ate away at her daily, but the compromising videos Jürgen held over her as a threat kept her silent. She knew that even the smallest act of rebellion could destroy her life, her marriage, and most importantly, her image in the eyes of their children. Every day, she played her part, losing herself a little more, forced to betray the man she had once loved without reservation.

As the days passed, the network tightened its grip on Leo with cold, methodical precision. It was no longer just a group of individuals working in the shadows; it became an omnipresent, suffocating force, controlling every detail of his life. Leo, for his part, struggled to breathe in this oppressive atmosphere, unable to comprehend that he was the target of a plan far larger and darker than anything he could have imagined.

PART 7:

The Psychological Decline of Leo

Chapters:

1. Leo loses confidence in himself

2. Troubling events and subtle manipulations

3. Eva plays her role despite herself

4. Leo struggles to understand what is happening

CHAPTER 1:

Leo loses confidence in himself

With the growing pressure exerted by the criminal network and the emotional isolation methodically orchestrated by Eva, Leo found himself spiraling downward. What once defined him, his confidence, determination, and clarity of mind, was slowly eroding. For the first time in years, Leo felt powerless, incapable of controlling what was happening in his own life.

The subtle manipulations Eva carried out relentlessly, under Jürgen's domination, were achieving their goal. Leo, a rational and thoughtful man who had built his success on solving complex problems, suddenly faced situations where none of his skills seemed sufficient. This loss of control over his own daily life created a void in his self-esteem, fueling insidious doubts.

Every interaction with Eva became an unsolvable puzzle. Her ambiguous responses, veiled reproaches, and distant behavior stirred growing unease in Leo. Where their conversations had once been warm and open, they were now filled with heavy silences and subtle accusations, designed to make him doubt his own mental stability. Eva didn't hesitate to suggest that Leo was imagining enemies, feeding his doubts about his lucidity. This strategy of gaslighting was devastating, forcing him to question his own judgment.

In his professional life, the repercussions of this destabilization were also apparent. Once highly effective and respected, Leo began making mistakes. Inexplicable misunderstandings with colleagues, missed deadlines, and contracts abruptly terminated without clear reasons piled up, deepening his loss of confidence. Each failure weakened him further, leading him to believe that he was the primary cause, incapable of keeping his life in order.

Faced with these repeated failures, Leo turned to Eva for support, but she was more distant than ever. She withheld any gestures of comfort, instead amplifying her subtle accusations, convincing him that he was losing control. Eva used every detail of their daily life to reinforce this belief, even going so far as to hide documents or discreetly sabotage his work, only to point out his supposed forgetfulness afterward. Powerless against this accumulation of small betrayals, Leo internalized Eva's words, doubting his ability to remember things.

Unable to find help or even someone to confide in about his distress, Leo felt his world crumble a little more each day. The criminal network, using Eva as its voice, worked to detach him from his certainties, his foundations, and his convictions. Once a man who saw himself as a pillar for his family and a leader in his work, Leo now viewed himself as a failing man, powerless against difficulties he could no longer comprehend.

This overwhelming doubt left Leo increasingly isolated. His once-unshakable self-confidence was gradually replaced by endless questions. He felt betrayed by an invisible, intangible source, a sinister force draining him of all energy. Leo was lost, unable to find logic in his descent into despair, let alone imagine that the network had orchestrated this slow and painful destruction.

As doubt grew within him, Leo sank further and further, unable to see a way out of this vicious cycle.

CHAPTER 2:

Troubling events and subtle manipulations

Every day, Leo increasingly felt the strange dissonance invading his daily life. Subtle signs, initially imperceptible, began to accumulate, leaving a troubling imprint on his mind. What might seem trivial to an outsider took on an oppressive air of mystery for him. His personal belongings appeared to move on their own, files he was certain he had organized vanished only to reappear elsewhere, and important work calls seemed to have never been made.

Leo tried to rationalize. "Maybe I'm just too tired?" he thought, repeatedly offering himself logical explanations, trying to convince himself that everything was normal. But a small voice in his head whispered otherwise, reminding him that these "accidents" were far too frequent and unsettling to be mere coincidences.

Faced with these inexplicable situations, Eva remained impassive, sometimes observing with a faint glimmer of satisfaction veiled behind a façade of feigned compassion. "You're becoming so distracted, Leo," she would say softly, encouraging him to "take care of himself." Her words seemed full of concern, but Leo felt an acidic irony behind every syllable, slowly eating away at him. His own wife, whom he had loved deeply and trusted implicitly, was becoming his secret tormentor, sowing seeds of doubt in his mind.

The Ever-Present Doubt and Leo's Thoughts

In the solitude of his evenings, Leo wondered if he truly needed to consult someone. He caught himself staring at his own reflection, searching in his eyes for a truth that seemed elusive. "Am I losing my mind? Is all of this even real?" These questions looped endlessly in his thoughts, never finding answers. Even his work, once an escape, had become a source of confusion and stress. Emails vanished, important files were inexplicably sent to the wrong recipients, and Leo found himself fixing mistakes he couldn't even recall making.

Meanwhile, Eva carried on her role with relentless precision. She isolated Leo from his friends and family, portraying herself as the victim of a husband who was losing his grip on reality. She discreetly confided to their close ones her worries about his mental health. She locked conversations, intercepted messages, and sowed doubts among those who might have otherwise been Leo's allies. In doing so, she tightened her hold on him, ensuring that Leo had no support system to help him understand the manipulation he was suffering.

Leo's Silent Distress

Leo was beginning to realize that he had no more anchors. The world felt increasingly blurred, filled with heavy silences and looks that only deepened his unease. He wanted to confide in someone, to find someone who could assure him that this was all just a bad dream. But he was alone, isolated in a labyrinth with no exit, where every path he took led him back to his own doubts.

In this climate of constant manipulation, the criminal network ensured that every step of Leo's downfall was carefully orchestrated. Their actions, meticulously calculated, aimed to gradually dismantle all the confidence he once had in himself, turning him into a man plagued by doubt, unable to discern truth from illusion. And as Leo sank deeper each day, he remained unaware that he was the prey of a carefully woven trap set around him by those who wanted him to disappear without a trace.

CHAPTER 3:

Eva plays her role despite herself

Beneath the cold and calculating façade she displayed, Eva remained deeply tormented by the role the criminal network forced her to play. Her life, once governed by her own choices, had turned into a theater of manipulation where she was nothing more than a puppet for Jürgen and his accomplices. Every day, she felt herself reduced further to a mere spectator of her own downfall, as her gestures, words, and glances toward Leo became tools of his destruction.

Whenever she saw him walking through the house, burdened and consumed by doubts, a dull pain tightened her throat. She silently questioned how she had ended up here. How had she allowed herself to be trapped so completely? Memories surged in waves, recalling the promises of a faithful love, shared dreams, and moments of once-unbreakable closeness. But these memories, far from offering her solace, made her torment unbearable, as they underscored with painful clarity that she had become the instrument of a betrayal beyond her control.

Every command from Jürgen was an ordeal. With every cruel word she uttered to fuel Leo's doubts, she felt a part of herself fade away. She knew her sly remarks, prolonged silences, and constant refusals were eating away at Leo, but she had no choice but to obey. "You're worth nothing anymore, Eva," she repeated silently to herself, convinced she could never reclaim the person she once was.

The guilt consumed her slowly. After every interaction with Leo, she found herself alone, battling the overwhelming sense of powerlessness that gnawed at her. She wondered if she might have found the strength to stop it all. But the compromising images, a sword of Damocles hanging over her, paralyzed her. She couldn't risk losing everything, seeing her life exposed and publicly ruined. So, she continued, hoping without conviction that an escape might present itself.

Leo, meanwhile, remained blind to the depth of the conspiracy but felt something was deeply wrong. His wife, once so close, was now a stranger, an elusive figure as cold as she was distant. He wanted to understand, still hoped to reclaim the loving woman he had known, but every attempt to reach out was met with a wall of ice. Confusion compounded his pain, and he often wondered in silent despair: "Where is the woman I loved so much?"

Eva, playing her role to perfection, masked her despair. She stayed composed, obedient, carrying out her instructions to the letter while inwardly praying that Leo wouldn't see the anguish in her eyes. For despite the distance, despite the betrayal she was committing, a part of her still loved him. This contradiction, this impossible coexistence of love and self-loathing, was tearing her apart.

Thus, every interaction between them became a silent battle, where words and gestures revealed only part of the truth. Leo, lost in the spiral of manipulation, continued to search for answers, while Eva, powerless, became day by day the executioner of the man she once loved more than anything.

CHAPTER 4:

Leo struggles to understand what is happening

Leo was at a breaking point. He was trying with all his strength to grasp what was happening around him, but each day seemed to drag him deeper into darkness. The small inconsistencies in daily life, the subtle changes in his environment, and above all, Eva's distant and troubling behavior plunged him into an abyss of confusion. He had always been a man of logic, someone who relied on facts and evidence. Yet, in this situation, nothing seemed logical.

The sleepless nights were piling up. In the silence of the house, Leo tried to piece together the puzzle, searching for the starting point of this descent into hell. "Did I miss something?" he wondered, replaying in his mind the events of the past months, the conversations with Eva, the glances, the silences.

There was something sinister, a shadow looming, but every time he tried to identify it, it slipped away from him.

Leo recalled the early signs of change in Eva. His wife, once full of life and affection, seemed to withdraw, retreating into a cold and unpredictable shell. She avoided him, found excuses not to talk or share moments with him. When he dared to express his feelings, she reacted with unsettling abruptness, insisting that he was imagining things, that he was becoming paranoid. "Why is she reacting this way? What did I do to cause this distance?" These questions looped endlessly in his mind.

He also began noticing disturbing details in his daily life: documents he thought he had carefully stored reappeared in improbable places, messages seemed to vanish, appointments were mysteriously canceled without reason. "Is it me? Am I really losing my mind?" These doubts seeped into every aspect of his life, leading him to question even his most recent memories. Reality was slipping away, transforming into a web of uncertainties from which he could no longer escape.

And then there were the looks from his children, innocent gazes that, on some days, seemed tinged with mistrust. Leo wondered what Eva might be telling them to make them look at him this way, with a distance he had never known from them before. On several occasions, he tried to talk to them, to remind them of the happy moments they had shared as a family, but unease quickly settled in. Even his own children now seemed beyond his grasp.

For Leo, each day became a battle between reason and emotion. On one hand, his mind told him that something serious was happening, that he needed to stay vigilant to understand and thwart what was happening in the shadows. But on the other hand, his love for Eva and his fear of losing her paralyzed his judgment, clouding his ability to see the truth. "Maybe she just needs space. Maybe I'm being too demanding?" he murmured to himself, struggling to maintain a semblance of normalcy.

In the end, Leo was left with this nagging question that haunted him day and night: "Who is pulling the strings? And why?" But despite his desperate attempts to answer it, he felt that every step forward only led him back to his solitude, to an unbearable void of answers.

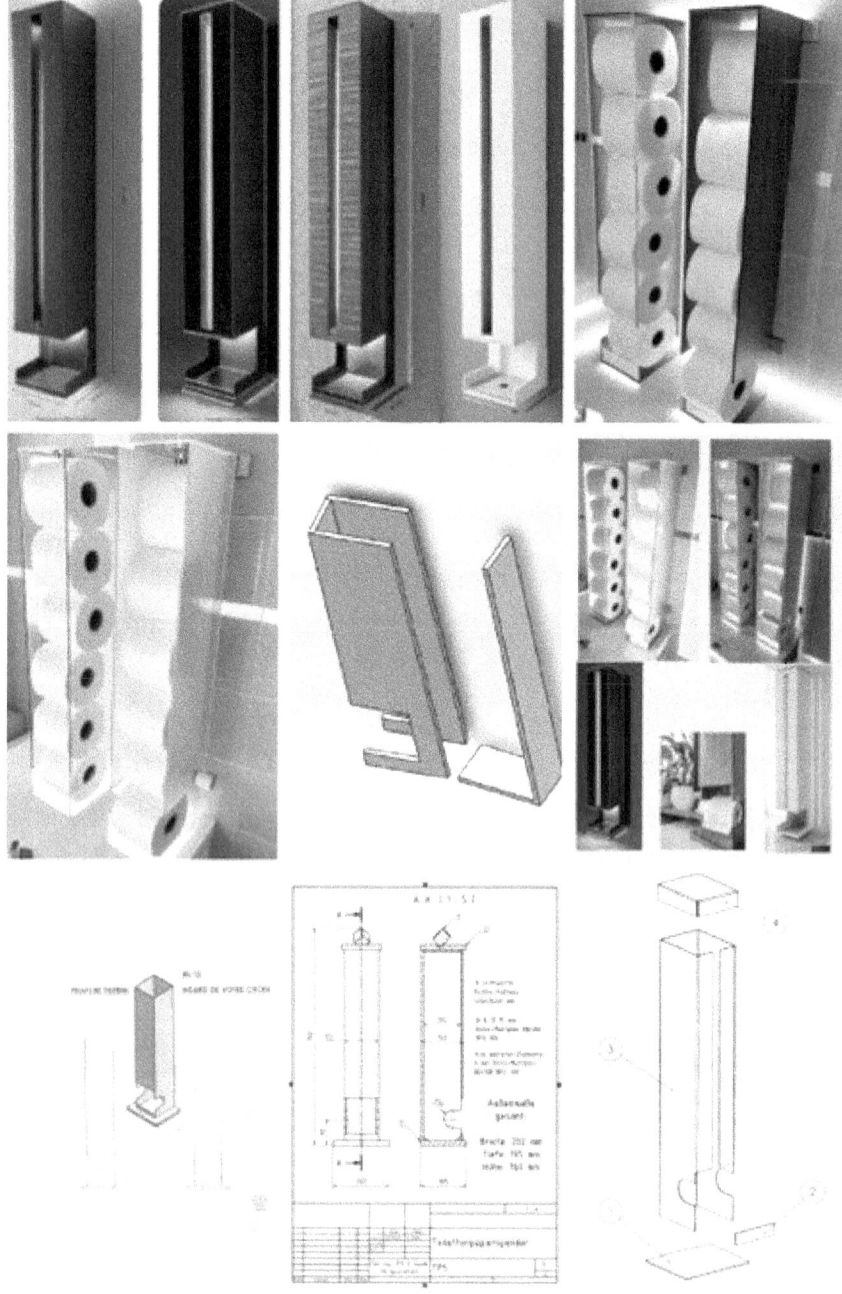

PART 8:

Love Turned Into a Weapon

Chapters:

1. Eva Becomes the Instrument of Leo's Destruction

2. The Orders She Must Follow

3. Leo Feels the Unease but Doesn't Understand

4. A Toxic Romantic Dynamic

CHAPTER 1:

Eva Becomes the Instrument of Leo's Destruction

Eva, once a devoted and loving wife, had transformed into a tool of destruction, wielded by the criminal network to break Leo. This gradual change, meticulously orchestrated, made her an obedient pawn in the hands of Jürgen and his allies, even as this transformation caused her profound inner torment. Under the pressure, manipulation, and threats of revealing compromising videos, Eva unwillingly became the central instrument in this cruel conspiracy.

Jürgen had established complete dominance over Eva. This was neither a romantic relationship nor an ordinary manipulation. Jürgen controlled her entirely, body and soul, slowly stripping her of her identity. This relationship of submission made Eva the perfect weapon against Leo, leaving her with no real possibility of escape. Trapped by her own mistakes, she saw no way out and followed every directive, no matter how cruel, in a desperate bid to salvage what remained of her reputation and integrity.

Under Jürgen's direct influence, Eva adopted behaviors that drove Leo into a spiral of doubt and self-deprecation. She learned to lace her words with disorienting insinuations, subtly planting the idea that he was losing his mind, that his thoughts were betraying him. When speaking to Leo, her statements were carefully crafted to suggest he needed help, as though he were suffering from schizophrenia or other mental disorders. This tactic, designed to erode Leo's trust in his own judgment, was executed with cold precision, though inwardly, Eva wrestled with the shame consuming her.

Beyond words, Eva's actions became increasingly treacherous. She moved objects around, hid certain items, and then blamed Leo for misplacing them. She exploited his fatigue and moral exhaustion to weaken him further, causing him to question his grasp on reality. With every move, Eva carried out the network's orders with chilling accuracy, as the chasm between her and Leo grew ever wider.

For the network, Eva's true power lay in her role as a seemingly caring and almost innocent wife. While Leo sensed a change, he could not fathom that his own wife was deliberately acting to push him toward ruin. This dissonance amplified the destructive impact of Eva's manipulations: even as doubts gnawed at him, Leo clung to the image of the woman he loved, unable to recognize her as the source of his destabilization.

The criminals' meticulously crafted plan found in Eva an unintentional but devastatingly effective accomplice. Knowing every one of Leo's vulnerabilities, she knew precisely where to press to cause the most pain. She alternated between icy detachment and feigned empathy, playing with his emotions to deepen his confusion. The more Eva acted this way, the deeper her guilt grew, but the constant threat of the videos and the total destruction of her life kept her trapped in this oppressive grip.

Deep down, a part of Eva still harbored feelings for Leo, and each act against him inflicted another wound on her. Yet, imprisoned in this forced role, she had no choice but to persist. Day by day, she became further entrenched as the network's instrument, not just to control Leo but to lead him toward his ultimate downfall.

CHAPTER 2:

The Orders She Must Follow

Eva, once a devoted and loving wife, was now completely under the control of the criminal network and Jürgen, the Agent Romeo. Every move, every word she spoke was meticulously directed to destroy Leo, while her own feelings of shame, fear, and despair became invisible chains binding her. Jürgen, merely a pawn in a much larger organization, exerted absolute domination over her, reinforcing his grip through precise, unrelenting orders that Eva had to follow without question or delay.

These orders were chillingly specific, designed to undermine Leo step by step without raising immediate suspicion from him or those around them. One of Jürgen's key directives was to isolate Leo from his friends and family. Any relationship perceived as a source of support for Leo had to be weakened or severed. With feigned concern and a counterfeit smile, Eva spread insidious rumors, fabricated lies, or subtly insinuated that Leo was unstable. She would sometimes unplug the home phone, intercept messages, or make unfounded accusations to widen the gap between Leo and his loved ones. Each manipulation contributed to Leo's growing isolation, leaving him increasingly vulnerable.

Simultaneously, Jürgen instructed Eva to deepen Leo's doubts about his own mental health. This directive was particularly cruel, as it sought to poison the confidence Leo had in himself. With a cruel finesse, Eva whispered seemingly caring but implicitly accusatory words into his ear. "You seem so tired, Leo. Don't you want to talk to someone about it?" or "Maybe you should consult a professional, just to be sure…" These remarks, innocuous on the surface, planted the idea in Leo's mind that he was losing his grip, slowly driving him toward an emotional dependency that Eva worked tirelessly to make indispensable. More and more confused, Leo clung to her, unaware that his greatest threat was the very person he believed to be his sole support.

Another aspect of the orders focused on sabotaging Leo's career. Ever the manipulator, Jürgen provided Eva with precise details about her husband's ongoing projects, pinpointing critical moments when a distraction could derail an important meeting or a key decision. Playing the role of a distracted wife or a hurried confidante, Eva subtly nudged Leo toward poor decisions, creating invisible obstacles in his professional path. She misplaced documents, swapped crucial information, or staged sly distractions at moments when Leo needed to focus most. Gradually, Leo's reputation eroded in the eyes of his colleagues and partners, and his self-assurance began to waver.

Jürgen's control over Eva extended to more sordid and humiliating commands, aimed at breaking her will entirely. Beyond manipulating her relationship with Leo, he forced her into degrading encounters with other members of the network, subjecting her to unimaginable humiliations. Whenever she thought she had hit rock bottom, Jürgen reminded her of the threat posed by the compromising videos. These recordings, wielded as leverage to ensure her obedience, became the chain that prevented her from fleeing, confessing the truth to Leo, or rebelling against this destructive hold.

As days turned into weeks, Eva found herself trapped in the role of an unwilling executioner, losing every part of what made her a loving wife and trustworthy person. She obeyed every command with chilling precision, fully aware that the slightest misstep could provoke Jürgen's wrath. Her fear and shame consumed her, leaving no room for rebellion.

For Eva, the situation had become a prison with no escape, her self-loathing buried under the constant fear of losing everything she held dear. She no longer dared to imagine a way out, as every attempt at resistance only tightened Jürgen's grip. The orders were clear and relentless: Leo had to be destroyed, not by an external enemy, but from within, by the one person in whom he had placed all his trust.

CHAPTER 3:

Leo Feels the Unease but Doesn't Understand

Leo was beginning to lose himself in a haze of contradictory feelings and unanswered suspicions. Everything felt slightly off, as though his life had veered from its natural course. Each moment with Eva, once a source of comfort and closeness, now carried an unexplained tension. He couldn't pinpoint the reason, but he felt increasingly like a stranger in his own home, where Eva embodied both familiarity and distance. This strangeness became an enigma, a puzzle for which he had no pieces to even guess at the image.

In their conversations, Eva's words carried a cold, heavy ambiguity. Every seemingly innocuous remark was tinged with an undertone that Leo couldn't fully grasp. He tried to find logic, a rational explanation, but every time he thought he was getting closer to the truth, it slipped away like a mirage in the desert. Eva's once-kind demeanor had morphed into a strange game of masks and silences. She would tell him he was becoming too stressed, that he was overreacting, but deep down, Leo felt he wasn't the sole cause of their growing distance.

This constant uncertainty affected him far beyond his personal life. At work, where he had built a reputation for precision and reliability, he found himself increasingly plagued by oversights and mistakes. Projects fell apart, crucial appointments slipped through his fingers, and each time, he blamed himself more. He felt like a shadow of his former self, losing his grip on responsibilities that had once seemed straightforward and natural.

The network had masterfully orchestrated this psychological war, exploiting his trust in Eva to make her the instrument of his confusion. The manipulations were so subtle that he couldn't identify their source, much less understand they came from the person he loved. By playing the role of a misunderstood wife, Eva ensured that Leo, burdened with guilt and doubt, continued to lower his defenses. And while Leo sensed, in some vague way, that his world was unraveling, he could never have imagined that this silent disintegration was caused by the one he trusted most.

Each day, Leo wrestled with an invisible internal struggle, unaware of the enemy lurking in the shadows, wearing the face of the woman he once believed he knew better than himself.

CHAPTER 4:

A Toxic Romantic Dynamic

Under the influence of the criminal network, Eva had become a version of herself that Leo no longer recognized, transforming their home into a psychological battleground where every interaction was fraught with insidious and painful tension. Their once trusting and close marriage had crumbled under the weight of manipulations orchestrated by Jürgen, the so-called Agent Romeo, who dictated Eva's every move. She was no longer the loving and warm woman Leo had known, but a compliant instrument of a network bent on breaking him emotionally.

The network's orders were meticulously calculated to dismantle Leo's stability, keeping him in a perpetual state of doubt and suffering. Sometimes, Eva would adopt a soft, almost soothing tone, giving him a fleeting glimpse of normalcy. She approached him with gestures reminiscent of their former intimacy, offering brief moments of tenderness. Clinging to the hope of rekindling their bond, Leo allowed himself to be lulled by these stolen moments, only to be met with abrupt changes in her behavior.

Reproaches and indifference followed every act of closeness, profoundly destabilizing Leo. This oscillation between affection and coldness plunged him into a spiral of emotional confusion, leaving him uncertain of what to expect next.

Acting on Jürgen's orders, Eva played on her own emotions and the memories of past happiness to manipulate Leo. In a calm yet calculated tone, she highlighted perceived flaws in him, accusing him of behaviors he didn't recognize. Leo began to question his own reality, convinced that he was the source of their discord. He swung between guilt and incomprehension, desperately searching for reasons behind her transformation.

Beyond words, Eva used their surroundings to intensify the atmosphere of doubt. Items she knew were important to Leo would mysteriously disappear, only to reappear in unusual places. These seemingly minor incidents were part of the methodical plan to weaken his mind. Leo started questioning whether he was truly losing his grip. Every conversation, every glance exchanged with Eva reinforced his belief that he might be slipping into paranoia or mental instability.

This cruel game of deception and duplicity slowly drained Leo of his strength. His love for Eva, which should have been his support, had turned into a devastating weapon wielded by the criminal network. The network understood that as long as Leo remained attached to her, they could manipulate him through her. Unaware of the betrayal unfolding, Leo found himself trapped by the very love that had once been his source of joy and was now the cause of his suffering.

Doubts gnawed at him to the point where he often wondered if he needed to question himself more deeply. Yet every attempt at reconciliation clashed with Eva's calculated coldness, as she rigorously followed Jürgen's directives. Leo clung to the belief that their relationship could still be salvaged, unknowingly feeding the trap set by his own feelings.

Thus, Leo navigated an environment he no longer recognized, imprisoned by his emotions and manipulated by unseen forces. The love that bound him to Eva had become his greatest vulnerability, a link the network exploited to carry out their plan to its conclusion. Every moment with her became a trial, a silent confrontation between a desperate man and a woman chained by cruel orders.

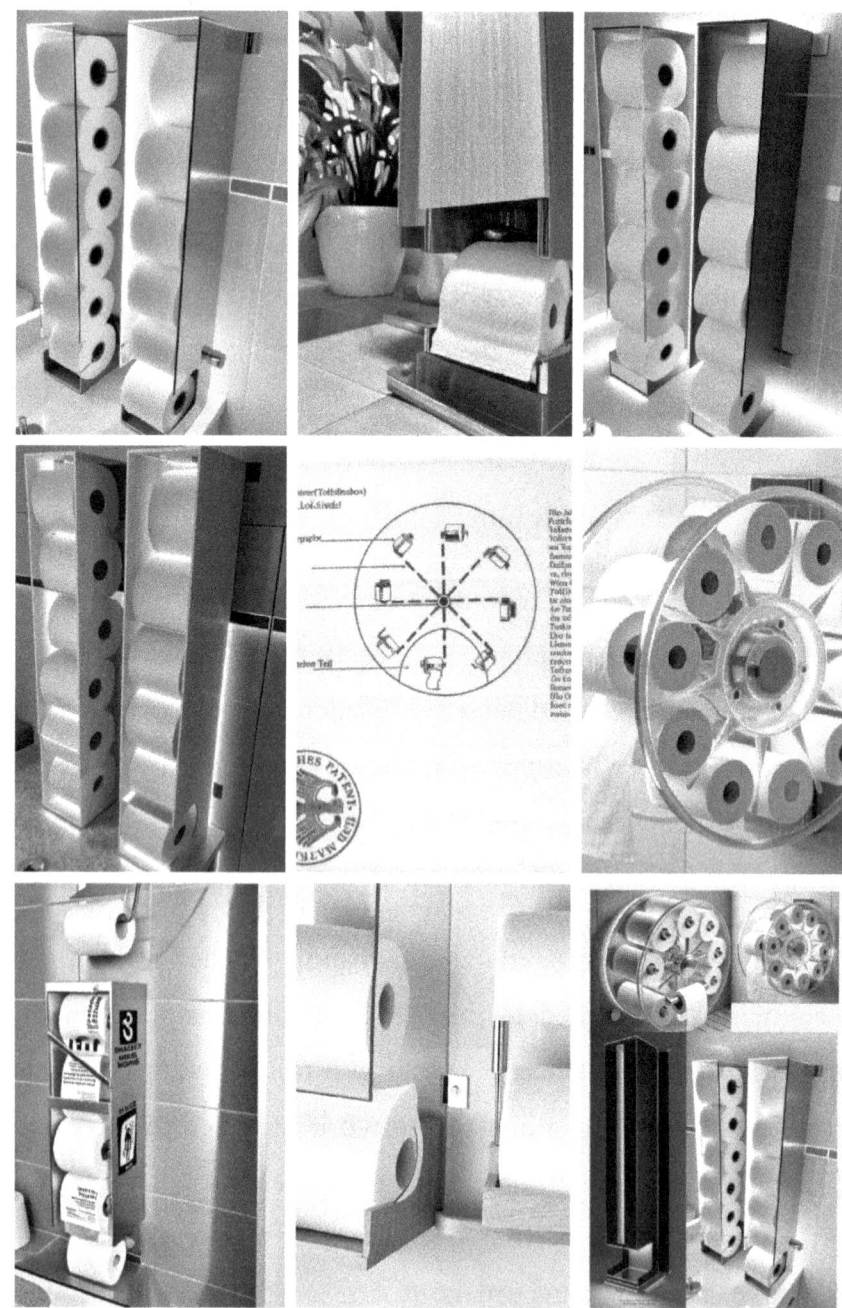

PART 9:

The Progressive Suffocation

Chapters:

1. The manipulation grows increasingly intense

2. Leo struggles to hold on to his reality

3. Eva's lies spiral out of control

4. The descent into darkness accelerates

CHAPTER 1:

The manipulation grows increasingly intense

Leo's situation worsened daily as the criminal network's meticulously orchestrated manipulation became increasingly intense and relentless. Eva, under Jürgen's control, continued her role in this plan, a role she despised but felt unable to escape. Each directive, chillingly precise, aimed to isolate Leo psychologically and erode his emotional stability without raising direct suspicions. The goal was simple: to destroy Leo methodically, ensuring he crumbled without ever understanding the cause.

The manipulations took on various forms. Under her manipulators' orders, Eva caused critical documents for Leo's projects to disappear, leading to errors in his work. She discreetly altered his schedule, causing him to miss crucial appointments. Bit by bit, Leo found himself facing professional failures he had never experienced before, each incident sowing deeper doubts about his own abilities. Once meticulous and organized, he now saw himself making inexplicable mistakes. These cascading professional failures devastated his self-esteem, reinforcing an inexplicable sense of incompetence.

Eva's influence extended to the private sphere as well. Phone calls Leo received were mysteriously cut off, and important messages seemed to vanish. Even critical letters went missing, sometimes torn apart before he could read them. His phone's SIM cards inexplicably deactivated, amplifying his sense of helplessness. Individually, these anomalies might have seemed like simple misunderstandings, but together they created a heavy atmosphere where Leo, despite his usual meticulousness, began to doubt his ability to manage his own daily life.

Aware of the psychological impact of these maneuvers, the network intensified the pressure. Eva alternated between displays of false affection and bouts of icy detachment. She cruelly dangled hope before Leo with small gestures of care, only to plunge him back into doubt and confusion with sharp accusations or trivial arguments that escalated disproportionately. These conflicts, often sparked by insignificant matters, left Leo in a state of confusion and emotional exhaustion. The oscillation between closeness and rejection kept Leo in a constant state of tension, pushing him to question his own mental health.

To exacerbate matters, Eva followed orders to sever Leo's ties with his social circle. Family dinner invitations were canceled without explanation, and messages from loved ones went unanswered. Opportunities to reconnect with friends disappeared one by one, leaving Leo increasingly isolated. This systematic distancing deprived him of external support, creating a vicious cycle where he could find neither help nor comfort. The network knew that the more isolated Leo became, the more vulnerable he would be to manipulation.

The manipulations reached a new peak when the network instructed Eva to involve the children in the destabilization process. Following Jürgen's orders, she subtly encouraged them to complain about Leo, voicing frustrations and fears they had never felt before. Leo, already mentally exhausted, was deeply hurt by these behaviors in his children. This attack targeted one of the most cherished aspects of his life: his role as a father. He began to see himself as a failure in his family, amplifying his feelings of guilt and helplessness.

Over time, Leo found himself entangled in an inescapable web woven by invisible yet omnipresent hands. Despite the isolation, confusion, and pain, he continued to hope, searching for a rational explanation. He couldn't grasp that all of this wasn't the result of his own mistakes but rather a carefully orchestrated plan by the criminal network. The network had, perhaps unknowingly, chosen an ideal target in Leo: a man who, when faced with the inexplicable, continued to blame himself, unable to see that the enemy was within his very home.

CHAPTER 2:

Leo Tries to Hold on to His Reality

Leo stared at his reflection in the bathroom mirror, his hands gripping the edge of the sink. His face, ravaged by sleepless nights and unrelenting anxiety, seemed both familiar and alien to him. His red, shadowed eyes brimmed with a despair he had never experienced before. The room, bathed in a pale, oppressive light, appeared strangely blurry, as though an intangible fog had invaded every corner.

The air was heavy, suffocating. Each breath was a deliberate effort, a struggle not to sink. Leo murmured to himself, almost as if to test his voice: "You're losing your mind, Leo." The words echoed in the silent room, laden with cruel irony. He needed to confirm that his voice still sounded real, that it still belonged to him.

For weeks, inexplicable events had haunted him. Objects he was certain he'd left in one spot would reappear elsewhere.

Important documents vanished from his desk, only to resurface days later in absurd locations. Strange, accusatory messages had appeared on his phone—messages Leo was certain he hadn't written. Yet their tone—subtly hostile—chilled him to the bone.

What Leo didn't realize was that these incidents were orchestrated by Eva. Operating from the shadows, she exploited his vulnerability. Often, she dissolved a sedative into his evening drink, ensuring a deep, unshakable sleep. Once unconscious, she would rearrange objects, plant the messages, and move documents to create calculated chaos. Every action was deliberate, meticulously designed to feed Leo's confusion and make him doubt his sanity.

But these disturbances paled in comparison to the living enigma Eva had become. Once his confidante and anchor, she now seemed like a foreign force—both familiar and utterly inaccessible. Her actions had become unpredictable, her words cutting, her silences colder than ever. Whenever Leo tried to share his growing unease, Eva would shrug dismissively with a forced smile that sent shivers down his spine.

"You're worrying over nothing, Leo," she often said. "It's just coincidences."

But this "nothing" had invaded every aspect of his life. Eva spoke in riddles, her words carefully chosen to further unbalance him. Her evasive remarks left him adrift in a mental fog, unable to discern truth from manipulation. It felt as though she were following a script he couldn't understand.

Eva's deliberate strategies to unsettle him became increasingly evident. She repeated absurd, almost obsessive behaviors—entering and exiting the bathroom ten times within an hour, pretending to take phone calls. When Leo cautiously asked if everything was okay, she lashed out: "Can't I have a moment to myself without you hovering? You're sick, Leo!"

Later, these incidents would be recounted to friends, twisted into anecdotes that painted Leo as a paranoid, oppressive husband. Gradually, he noticed the shifting glances of those around him, the skepticism and growing distance. Each subtle act of alienation felt like an invisible wound, deepening his despair.

What Leo still couldn't fully grasp was that all of this was part of a meticulously orchestrated strategy. An unseen force was at work, exploiting every crack in his psyche. The mafia, deeply embedded in administrative systems, employed subtle methods to break their victims. Ordinary actions, amplified through repeated manipulations, were designed to unnerve Leo until he reacted. And once he did, those reactions were used against him to discredit him further.

Leo couldn't bring himself to believe that Eva was complicit. His love for her was too profound, his moral grounding too strong to entertain such betrayal. Yet with each passing day, he couldn't deny that something sinister was at play. The reality he had known was crumbling, replaced by a world where nothing was certain.

As he sank deeper into his thoughts, the bathroom door abruptly opened. Eva stepped in, her face unreadable, frozen in an expression he couldn't decipher.

"What are you doing?" she asked, her voice taut and cold.

Leo didn't answer immediately. He continued staring at his reflection, searching for remnants of his identity in the face he no longer recognized.

"Just... trying to hold on to something," he finally murmured, his voice muffled by exhaustion.

Eva moved closer, her footsteps echoing like hammer blows in the silence. When she placed a cold hand on his shoulder, Leo felt a chilling jolt. The touch, far from comforting, felt like an anchor dragging him underwater.

"Sometimes it's better to forget," she whispered. "What's behind us doesn't matter anymore."

Leo turned to her, searching her eyes for anything—some clue, some emotion. But all he found was an impenetrable wall, a calculated opacity. Eva was a stranger now, someone familiar yet wholly unknown.

Yet, deep within Leo, a spark remained. Tiny, flickering, but undeniably alive. He realized he had to cling to it, no matter what. If he let that flame die, he knew he would never recover.

Gripping the sink edge with renewed determination, his knuckles whitened under the pressure.

"I'm not crazy," he thought. "Not yet."

As Eva left the room, a barely perceptible smile playing on her lips, Leo felt a chilling certainty: the battle for his reality was only just beginning.

CHAPTER 3:

Eva's lies spiral out of control

Leo's manipulation was turning into an increasingly complex trap as everything around him seemed to crumble. Doubts seeped into his daily life, threatening to sever the fragile thread that still connected him to reality. Although his rational mind suggested that something serious was spiraling out of his control, Leo resisted succumbing to paranoia. Instead, he tried to strengthen the aspects of his life he could still control, hoping these anchors would stabilize him.

Leo saw his work as an engineer as a refuge where logic and precision reigned supreme. Every project demanded his utmost concentration, and he channeled his worries into this work. But even in this sanctuary, the invisible sabotages orchestrated by Eva gradually undermined his balance. Mistakes, lost documents, and inexplicable delays cropped up incessantly. Leo found himself trapped in a vicious cycle: the more he clung to his work, the more manipulations intensified, pushing him to question his own efficiency.

The situation grew even more complicated in his family circle. Moments with his children, once a source of solace, became increasingly strained and distant. Under Jürgen's pressure, Eva sowed seeds of mistrust in their minds, emphasizing Leo's alleged shortcomings as a father. She subtly stoked conflicts, diverting the children's attention to foster doubt about him. Leo felt the chasm growing between them but couldn't understand its true origin. His attempts to rebuild natural connections were systematically sabotaged, as if every gesture of affection slipped out of reach.

In his despair, Leo clung to memories of his past, searching for proof of his strength and identity. He recalled moments of complicity with Eva and their shared life before this nightmare began. But the more he tried to hold onto these memories, the more distant and blurry they seemed, as though they belonged to someone else. These images eroded under the weight of manipulation, leaving him in a state of bitter nostalgia and helplessness.

Leo's mental and emotional confusion peaked whenever he tried to address these issues with Eva. In public, she played the role of a caring wife, but behind this facade, her actions were orchestrated to fuel his doubts. At times, she offered fleeting words of comfort, creating the illusion of normalcy for Leo. However, this kindness would quickly vanish, replaced by sharp reproaches and accusatory remarks that hit him hard.

Despite this constant onslaught of pressure and manipulation, Leo did not give up. Each day, he sought to find new footholds, reasons to believe he could still turn things around. In moments of solitude, he took long walks, attempting to find inner peace and clarity. Yet these efforts were in vain, as every step forward seemed to lead him to another dead end. Memories of his past intertwined with present doubts, leaving him oscillating between the certainty of a conspiracy and the fear of descending into madness.

Thus, Leo battled daily for his reality, his love for Eva and his children serving as his last glimmers of hope. But without knowing it, he was struggling within a trap, where every attempt to understand only seemed to advance the criminal network's plans.

As the manipulation orchestrated by Jürgen and the criminal network intensified, Eva's lies evolved into a complex labyrinth of deceptions, gradually spiraling out of control. What had begun as simple evasions to protect her secrets grew into an inextricable web of contradictions and fabrications, threatening to engulf both her relationship with Leo and her mental stability.

Initially, Eva lied to avoid compromising her relationship with Leo, hoping each small lie would be enough to safeguard her secrets. However, the network's demands kept increasing, and each new mission imposed by Jürgen required increasingly elaborate stories. Soon, omissions and half-truths were no longer sufficient. She had to create entire narratives to justify her absences, expenditures, and suspicious behavior. Her mind became cornered by the necessity of maintaining her role while losing any trace of sincerity in her words.

Contradictions piled up, and Eva felt her mind fragmenting under the constant pressure of deception. She invented excuses to explain her prolonged absences: endless errands, visits to fictitious friends, impromptu activities, but her explanations never quite added up. Leo, for his part, noticed these inconsistencies and tried to make sense of them. Whenever he confronted her, Eva skillfully turned the situation around, making him doubt his own memories and perceptions, exploiting his rational mind to convince him he was imagining problems where none existed.

Leo, aware that something eluded his understanding, mentally noted these inconsistencies, even though tangible evidence remained elusive. Occasionally, while discreetly searching through Eva's belongings, he stumbled upon troubling clues, though insufficient to accuse her directly. These discoveries deepened his confusion, intensifying his sense of betrayal without providing clear answers. He oscillated between anger and doubt, seeking rational explanations for what increasingly seemed irrational.

Eva's lies also corroded her psyche. Lying constantly to herself to justify her actions, she found herself caught in a spiral of self-destruction. Her mental health deteriorated under the weight of her double life. This omnipresent deception consumed her thoughts, blurred her ability to distinguish truth from fiction, and plunged her into relentless confusion. Moments of lucidity, where she remembered who she truly was, became increasingly rare. In her dreams, fragments of truth and lies intermingled, haunting her like ghosts she could not escape.

Meanwhile, Jürgen observed this deterioration closely. The deeper Eva sank into her lies, the more she depended on him to maintain control. Every act of deception further bound her to him, making her increasingly vulnerable to his manipulations. The network exploited this fragility to tighten its grip, knowing that any attempt to restore the truth would irrevocably destroy her life with Leo and her social image. Jürgen merely had to pull the strings of this desperate puppet to make her act increasingly against her own interests, trapping her in a vicious cycle of deceit.

Eva's lies eventually spiraled beyond her control. She no longer knew how to navigate the web she had helped weave. The criminal network, by orchestrating this perverse manipulation, achieved a major goal: Eva, now their instrument of deceit, was cornered by her own words. The truth, buried under so many falsehoods, dissolved entirely, leaving behind an abyss of uncontrollable lies.

CHAPTER 4:

The descent into darkness accelerates

Leo's tragedy plunged into even darker depths as the destruction orchestrated by the criminal network accelerated, tightening inexorably around him and Eva. The psychological tension, already unbearable, evolved into a daily nightmare, a descent into hell where Leo lost his bearings and Eva her identity.

For Leo, every aspect of his life was affected. This vicious manipulation didn't just create emotional distance; it infiltrated his thoughts, emotions, and most deeply held beliefs. There was no escape or refuge, not even in his own mind. He increasingly felt disconnected from reality, unable to distinguish what was real from what had been meticulously orchestrated. Struggling to find a rational explanation for his growing confusion, everything around him turned hostile and oppressive. The home, once a symbol of comfort and safety, had transformed into a place of anxiety where every interaction with Eva deepened his isolation and despair.

Eva, on the other hand, had lost all autonomy. Jürgen and the network held her tightly in their grasp, forcing her to play a role she no longer recognized. She was instrumentalized, reduced to a puppet, compelled to participate in actions that disgusted her, making her an unwilling accomplice in Leo's destruction. Jürgen exploited this control to push Eva to her psychological limits, involving her in acts she would never have imagined. Their relationship had become a nightmarish prison where Jürgen imposed humiliations and degradations, making any attempt at retreat impossible for Eva.

Jürgen, the "Agent Roméo," had total control over her, turning her into an obedient puppet. Her will had been shattered, and she was used not only to manipulate Leo but also to satisfy the whims and fantasies of Jürgen and his accomplices. The relationship between them was no longer one of lover and mistress but master and slave. Jürgen regularly delivered her to other men or women, forcing her into behaviors she would never have considered. Eva lived in shame and self-loathing, unable to escape this vicious circle.

The lies she had woven around Leo had tangled into an inextricable web, to the point that she herself lost track of them. She could no longer distinguish truth from falsehood, and each encounter, each interaction became an increasingly desperate exercise in concealment. Her own words and actions had become traps that imprisoned her in this network of deception, leaving her no choice but to continue playing this destructive role, no matter the cost.

For Leo, this intensification of manipulation marked the breaking point. The network had carefully prepared every step, and each of Eva's lies, each additional manipulation, became another brick in the wall isolating him entirely from reality and the people he loved. His attempts to regain mental stability, to analyze and understand what he was experiencing, were exhausted by the relentless attacks. He had no anchor left, and this descent, so meticulously orchestrated, dragged him into an abyss of confusion and despair.

The network, sensing that its prey was on the verge of breaking, tightened its grip with devastating determination. It knew the moment was near, that Leo was teetering on the edge of collapse. The tension of this psychological drama reached its climax as Leo, on the brink of the abyss, made one final attempt to comprehend the incomprehensible, searching for a fragment of clarity in what had become pure chaos.

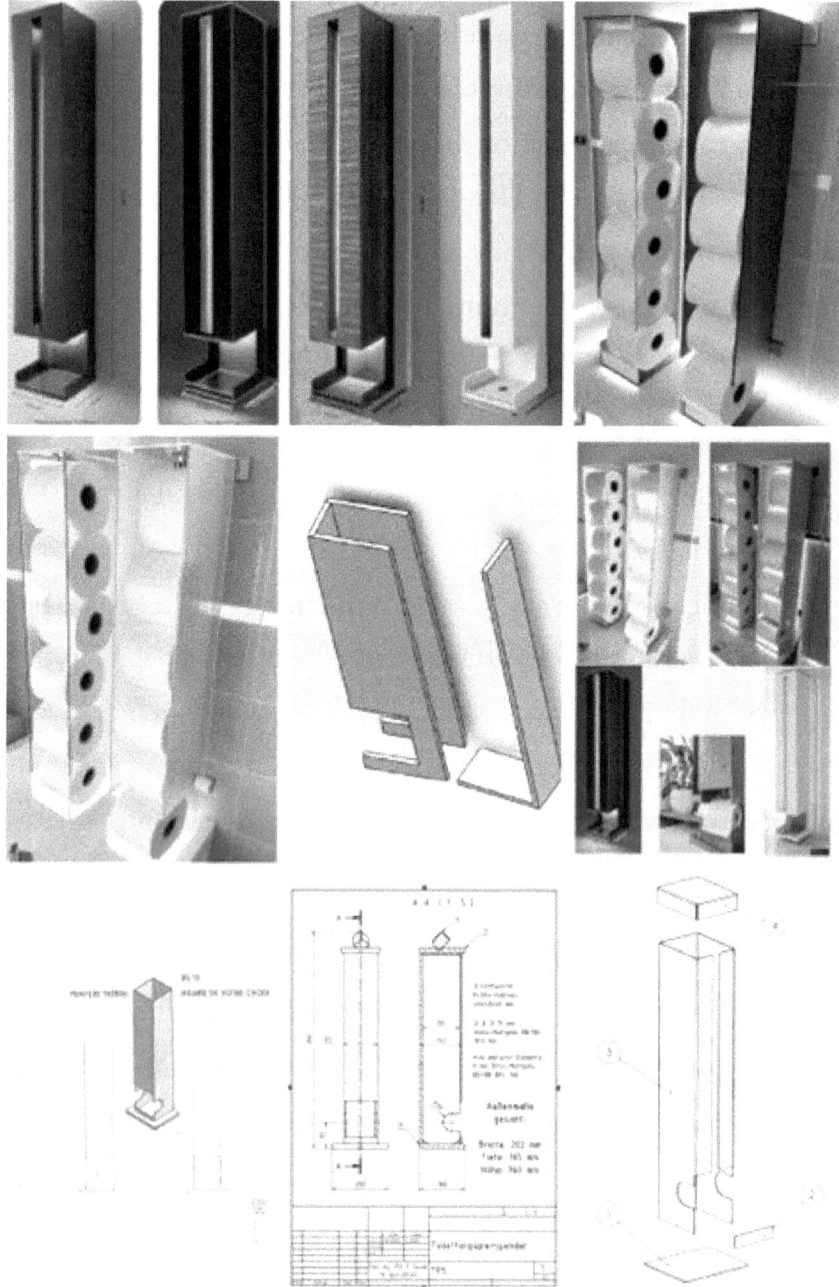

PART 10:

The Invisible Network

Chapters:

1. The Puppet Masters Pulling the Strings

2. Eva Under Complete Control

3. Leo Increasingly Isolated

4. The Imminence of the Breaking Point

CHAPTER 1:

The Puppet Masters Pulling the Strings

As the trap tightened, the true architects behind Leo's downfall emerged as powerful and enigmatic figures, operating from the shadows with calculated precision. Unlike Jürgen, the "Agent Romeo," who was ruthless yet merely a pawn in this grand conspiracy, the real masterminds stood apart through their influence and Machiavellian strategy.

These shadowy figures were not mere petty criminals but part of a deeply entrenched network within society. Their reach extended far beyond Leo and Eva's private sphere, infiltrating critical domains such as politics, business, and even the judiciary. With their far-reaching influence, they acted with impunity, protected by layers of anonymity, aliases, and well-placed accomplices. Each of their moves was carefully planned to dismantle Leo without raising any suspicion. This insidious control allowed them to observe, as invisible spectators, the gradual demise of their victim.

They exploited human vulnerabilities with extraordinary skill. In Leo's case, Eva served as their gateway, once a loyal wife, but vulnerable due to her emotional flaws and unmet needs. Once Eva fell under their control, they transformed her into a pawn, an emotional weapon used to strike Leo where it hurt most: his heart, his personal life, and his family.

Their hold was rooted in fear, an omnipresent psychological terror. The incriminating videos of Eva, tangible evidence that could instantly ruin her life and Leo's, hung over her like the sword of Damocles. Eva knew any act of defiance would be met not with physical violence but with a psychological assault far more devastating: the revelation of her betrayal. Shame, fear of losing her marriage, her reputation, and even her family's safety kept her bound, unable to break free from this malevolent grip.

For Leo, these oppressive forces remained unseen. The growing challenges in his professional life, lost contracts, severed collaborations, persistent rumors, seemed to arise out of nowhere, a chain of inexplicable failures plunging him deeper into self-doubt. Every setback at work, every new conflict, and every disappointment strengthened his sense of helplessness, slowly eroding him from within.

The masterminds didn't work alone. Surrounding them was a network of loyal individuals, each fulfilling a specific role, Jürgen, of course, but also field agents, discreet informants, corrupt businesspeople, and influential officials who served the network's goals, sometimes for profit, sometimes out of fear. Through this intricate web, they wove an inescapable trap around Leo, isolating him without his awareness.

The network's strategy was chillingly subtle: to ensure Leo's downfall occurred without a chance for defense, to make his destruction gradual and inevitable so that he would lose faith in his loved ones, his perception of reality, and ultimately in himself. Eva, consumed by shame and helplessness, remained unable to break the silence, trapped by a fear far greater than any instinct for emotional survival. As for Leo, he was isolated, cut off from supportive relationships, and weakened by increasingly inexplicable situations.

The puppet masters were merciless marionettists, waiting patiently yet pitilessly for their victim to reach a breaking point. They knew that when he collapsed, there would be no escape, no way back, marking a complete and decisive victory for their diabolical conspiracy.

CHAPTER 2:

Eva Under Complete Control

Eva had become a complete puppet, a mere extension of the will of the blackmailers who controlled her entirely. Once, she had clung to faint traces of resistance, a dim hope of preserving some part of herself; but that faint glimmer of freedom had been utterly extinguished. The blackmailers, through Jürgen, had systematically enslaved her mind and body, building an invisible prison around her from which she saw no escape.

Behind every movement, every word she directed at Leo, now lay an order dictated by the criminal network. This was no longer mere emotional or psychological manipulation but total domination. Jürgen, once a seducer, had transformed into a true oppressor. He was no longer just her lover or manipulator; he had become the master of her life, imposing his demands and whims without the slightest compassion.

Worse still, he was no longer content with exploiting Eva for his own desires. He regularly delivered her to other influential members of the network, using her to satisfy the fantasies of those pulling the strings from the shadows.

This situation plunged Eva into an abyss of constant terror. Each day, she sank further into submission, unable to break the invisible chains binding her to this destructive network. She no longer saw any hope of escaping this nightmare. The compromising videos, which had initially served as leverage to control her, were now just one of many threats wielded over her. Now, the blackmailers held every aspect of her life, every secret and every weakness, making her feel trapped in an inescapable system where the slightest rebellion would mean the complete collapse of her world.

This total control had profound effects on Eva's psyche. She felt broken, not only as a woman but as a human being. Despite everything, an attachment to Leo lingered within her, but this love had become a twisted emotion, tangled with insurmountable guilt and self-hatred. Every action, every lie, reminded her of the betrayal she was perpetuating, and she lived in self-loathing, trapped in this role of a destructive instrument she could no longer control.

The blackmailers, as masters of manipulation, knew how to exploit her emotions and guilt to keep her compliant. At times, they promised her liberation if she obeyed blindly; at others, they plunged her into deeper despair by reminding her that any attempt at rebellion would bring irreversible consequences. Jürgen, who served as the link between Eva and the network, skillfully alternated between threats and false promises, sometimes presenting himself as her only support in this hell, though he was merely another cog in her subjugation.

The network had thus transformed Eva into a being without agency, a puppet whose every move served a calculated purpose. They had stripped her of autonomy, reducing her to a pawn whose sole function was to obey, manipulate, and serve interests far greater than her own suffering. Eva was no longer anything more than a tool on the complex chessboard of this conspiracy, trapped in a nightmare from which she could neither escape nor denounce.

CHAPTER 3:

Leo Increasingly Isolated

As the manipulation intensified, Leo's isolation turned into a meticulously designed trap by the blackmailers, stripping him of any emotional or social support. This methodical destruction wasn't merely aimed at weakening him mentally, it sought to ensure that Leo had no refuge or comfort from anyone. Gradually, he watched all his anchors disintegrate, his world fragment, and his relationships deteriorate.

Eva, now imprisoned in her role under Jürgen's and the criminal network's control, actively contributed to this isolation. Her emotional distance, cold and unpredictable behavior, made communication nearly impossible for Leo. Once his anchor and ally, Eva had transformed into a source of pain. Her evasive glances, calculated silences, and false accusations plunged Leo into a constant state of anxiety. He tried to hold on to her but repeatedly encountered a wall of indifference, or worse, contempt. The pain of no longer recognizing the woman he had loved in Eva added an unbearable weight to his despair.

The blackmailers knew isolating Leo from his children, family, and close friends was crucial. Through subtle directives, they pushed Eva to sow seeds of doubt in the minds of their children and extended family. With sly skill, she painted Leo as someone disturbed, mentally fragile, or even dangerous. Innocuous-seeming comments, small insinuations that Leo was unpredictable or unstable, gradually took root in the minds of those around him. The children, influenced by these toxic whispers, began looking at their father with silent suspicion, further amplifying Leo's emotional burden.

This climate of doubt and suspicion extended to his friendships as well. Leo noticed that relationships he had once considered strong began to fray. Calls became infrequent, conversations more superficial, and Leo felt the growing distance without understanding why. Invitations that used to be regular suddenly ceased. His attempts to open up, to reconnect with his loved ones, were met with palpable discomfort, or worse, awkward silences. Every unraveling connection fed his sense of abandonment, betrayal, and, most painfully, loneliness. He could sense, without concrete proof, that something was orchestrating his exclusion from those he cared about.

Leo's isolation wasn't confined to his personal life. Strange incidents in his professional sphere multiplied, undermining his credibility and reputation. Business partners withdrew without reason, colleagues appeared distrustful, and contracts were abruptly canceled. These events eroded his confidence in himself and his professional environment. He felt constantly betrayed, as if every aspect of his once well-managed life was slipping beyond his control. This accumulation of setbacks overwhelmed him to the point of questioning his own worth and identity.

Leo's isolation reached unbearable proportions. Every attempt to seek support ended in rejection or increased distance. The isolation deepened, fueled by the criminal network's carefully orchestrated manipulations. Cornered, Leo even began to question whether he was responsible for the spiral of mistrust surrounding him. His rational mind started to waver, unable to make sense of the events and behaviors encircling him. He doubted his perceptions, sometimes imagining it was all a product of his own mind, only to be reminded that, regardless of the cause, the feeling of abandonment and solitude was all too real.

As the network tightened its grip, Leo found himself without allies, without anchors, and, most critically, without confidence in himself.

CHAPTER 4:

The Imminence of the Breaking Point

As the manipulations of the criminal network reached their peak, Leo inched dangerously close to his breaking point, a threshold beyond which he might collapse entirely. Every facet of his life seemed to turn against him, and every new interaction with Eva or professional setback nudged him closer to this fateful limit.

Eva, now under the absolute control of Jürgen and the network, played her role with chilling precision, oscillating between cold indifference and deceptive compassion that plunged Leo into unbearable confusion. Those fleeting moments when she seemed willing to reconcile were immediately followed by crises and destabilizing reproaches, methodically chipping away at Leo's psychological resilience. This calculated alternation rendered all of Leo's attempts to salvage their relationship not only futile but destructive. His determination to understand and resolve their conflicts dragged him deeper into the complex web of manipulations orchestrated by the network.

Despite his efforts to remain lucid, Leo felt his life crumbling before his eyes. His once-solid, rational, and methodical mind was now consumed by doubt, undermined by Eva's constant accusations and the apparent inconsistencies in his own perception of reality. The criminal network exploited this newfound fragility, amplifying his disorientation. Every interaction with Eva became a mental trap, causing him to question his memories, his logic, and even his identity.

The near-unbearable pressures extended beyond his marriage. Leo, already stripped of familial and social support by the network's manipulations, now saw his professional relationships deteriorate under the same toxic influence. Projects that had once been a source of pride slipped from his grasp, tainted by inexplicable errors and unexpected failures. Each professional setback and blow to his reputation deepened his feelings of personal failure and worthlessness, tightening the downward spiral that ensnared him.

Leo's isolation reached new heights. As the criminal network tightened its grip, even his professional allies distanced themselves from him. A longtime business partner, Olivier S., confessed during a tense meeting that he had been forced to sever ties with Leo. Although unable to provide details, he admitted receiving anonymous threats warning him against any association with Leo, under penalty of severe retaliation. Stunned by this revelation, Leo understood these intimidations were no coincidence but part of the network's grand plan to dismantle his life.

A similar incident occurred with another partner based in Spain, who abruptly ended their successful collaboration. In a cryptic message, the partner explained he could not jeopardize his family's safety by maintaining their partnership. These withdrawals were further evidence of the network's use of threats and intimidation to strip Leo of professional support, leaving him increasingly vulnerable.

Meanwhile, Eva continued her duplicitous role during business dinners and professional events, subtly contributing to Leo's deteriorating reputation. With calculated mastery, she injected subtle but defamatory remarks, hinting at Leo's alleged instability or "challenging" professional behavior. She presented herself as a "concerned" wife, playing on the empathy of her audience. These insinuations took root in the minds of Leo's potential partners, sowing enough doubt to dissuade them from collaborating with him.

These coordinated maneuvers further isolated Leo, targeting the core of his professional network. Not only was he losing valuable partnerships, but he was also becoming a pariah in his own field. His credibility, slowly eroded, was compromised daily by a web of lies and intimidation. Faced with this reality, Leo no longer knew whom to turn to or how to regain the stability he had once built.

Eva, meanwhile, exploited Leo's vulnerabilities to push him toward self-destructive behavior. By stoking his guilt, she subtly encouraged him to seek solace in harmful habits like alcohol or impulsive reactions that further jeopardized his career and image. This insidious strategy was integral to the network's plan: not only to isolate and weaken Leo but also to incite him to discredit himself, making his downfall appear entirely self-inflicted.

The blackmailers observed this decline with satisfaction, knowing Leo was approaching his breaking point. They were in no hurry, confident that the slow pace of his collapse would ensure their ultimate victory. The mental destruction they inflicted was designed to bring Leo to a state where recovery was impossible. Isolated, betrayed by his wife, and consumed by self-doubt, Leo had become the perfect target, with no means to fight back or escape the invisible trap.

With each passing day, the noose tightened around Leo. His relentless struggle to understand what was happening clashed against walls of incomprehension and loneliness. He felt the imminence of his fall yet refused to give up, holding out hope for a solution, a way to escape this slow descent into despair. However, the blackmailers, still lurking in the shadows, waited patiently, confident that the moment of his downfall was near and that their meticulously crafted plan would soon reach its culmination.

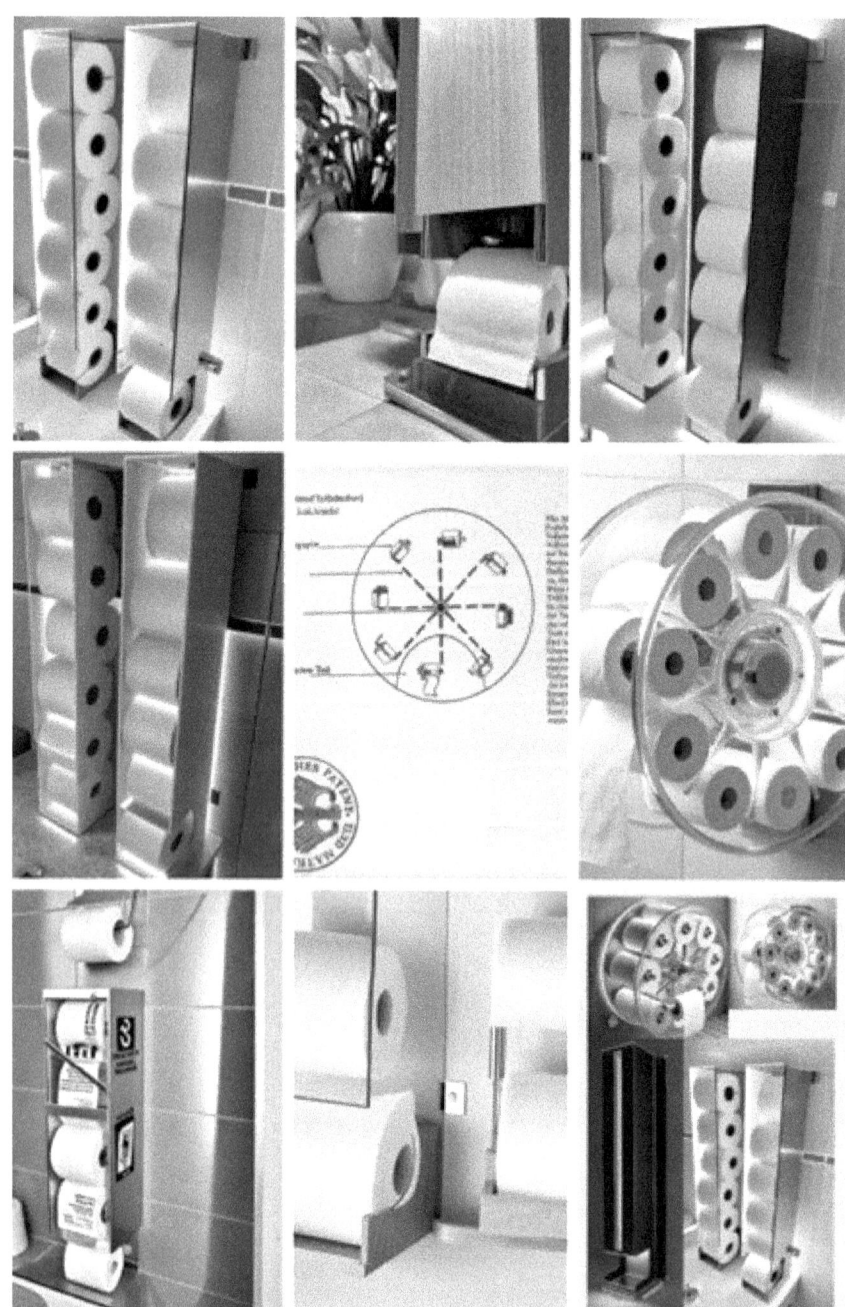

PART 11:

The Brutal Awakening

Chapters:

1. Leo Discovers Troubling Clues
2. The Truth About the Assassination Attempts Emerges
3. Eva: Both Victim and Accomplice
4. The Inevitable Confrontation

CHAPTER 1:

Leo Discovers Troubling Clues

At this crucial moment, Leo finally began piecing together a puzzle far more complex than he had ever imagined. What had for months seemed like fleeting suspicions and troubling coincidences transformed into a sequence of tangible revelations, marking the beginning of a painful but necessary awakening.

It started with resurfacing memories, moments when Eva appeared deeply engrossed in her thoughts, taking calls she would never answer in his presence or hastily ending them when he approached. Faces of strangers and unexpected encounters also came to mind, once dismissed as innocuous but now laden with heavier implications: Eva wasn't merely distracted; she was connected to a parallel reality she had meticulously concealed.

Leo's discoveries intensified when he stumbled upon a hotel receipt, an upscale location where Eva had no plausible reason to be. Carelessly left behind by her, the receipt was dated to a period when she had claimed family obligations. This seemingly innocuous slip of paper was the first concrete evidence of something sinister brewing in the shadows. Adding to this was Leo's unsettling memory of Jürgen's car, spotted multiple times near their home. Gradually, he began to see every detail, every odd moment, as part of a carefully orchestrated plan, with Eva and Jürgen as its main players.

Driven by an urgent need to uncover the truth, Leo scrutinized their bank statements, documents he had always entrusted to Eva without question. What he found shook him: a series of suspicious transactions, significant sums spent at places that didn't align with her explanations. These payments, often made during her so-called outings with the children or routine errands, deepened his doubts and exposed the extent of her hidden secrets.

While searching their home, Leo discovered a hidden phone in a drawer belonging to Eva. This phone, one he had never seen or accessed, was a shocking revelation. Within it, he found encrypted exchanges with unknown numbers. The messages, often brief and coded, referenced meetings and demands he couldn't immediately decipher but which hinted at a much broader and more sinister collaboration than he had imagined. This was no longer a matter of distrust; it was the unmasking of a conspiracy in which Eva played an active role, working hand-in-hand with forces intent on his destruction.

Faced with these undeniable truths, Leo felt a storm of emotions raging within him. The love he had once felt for Eva was consumed by a wave of anger and betrayal. He realized that what he had believed to be marital difficulties was, in fact, a smokescreen for a meticulously planned effort to dismantle him mentally, professionally, and emotionally.

Though shaken and deeply hurt, Leo understood the urgency of the situation. These revelations demanded immediate action before the trap closed completely around him. For the first time since his descent into this nightmare, Leo saw clearly that his enemy was neither madness nor misfortune, but a calculated network determined to destroy him. With time running out, he resolved to confront this newfound truth head-on, knowing that this battle would require every ounce of strength to salvage what remained of his life and identity.

CHAPTER 2:

The Truth About the Assassination Attempts Emerges

At the height of his anxieties, Leo received an anonymous note slipped under the door of his office. The message was as cryptic as it was alarming: "Be careful, a network is watching you. They've failed but won't stop. Beware of those who approach you with business offers." This warning, both vague and precise, triggered deep doubts within Leo. For the first time, he began to consider that the series of misfortunes in his life might not be random occurrences but part of a deliberate scheme aimed at destroying him.

Leo immediately recalled the troubling incidents that had marked the past months: the sudden failure of his car brakes, the cigarette butt placed under his vehicle seemingly to start a fire, and the near-miss accident involving Annika H. At the time, Leo had dismissed these events as bad luck. But the note changed everything. He now understood that these were not accidents but veiled assassination attempts, confirming that he faced a danger far greater than he had imagined.

Among his recent connections, one name stood out: Leander P., a millionaire engineer well-regarded in the industrial sector. Leander had entered Leo's life shortly after several of these incidents, offering him a business opportunity that had initially seemed genuine and enticing. There had been nothing suspicious in Leander's demeanor; his interest in Leo's innovations and his amicable behavior appeared above reproach. However, in the climate of mistrust Leo now found himself in, he couldn't ignore a nagging sense of doubt about Leander, even as he realized there was no concrete reason to justify it, yet.

Re-reading the note, Leo focused on the phrase "business offers." It gained particular significance, planting a seed of suspicion in his mind. What if Leander was more than just a potential investor? At this point, Leo had no direct evidence to accuse anyone, but he felt compelled to scrutinize every relationship, even one as seemingly trustworthy as Leander's.

Driven by an urgent need for clarity, Leo began to carefully examine his memories and interactions with Leander. He started noticing troubling coincidences between their meetings and the incidents. Timelines that once seemed insignificant now took on a more sinister pattern. The proximity of these events led him to suspect that Leander might be a cog in the intricate machinery of this conspiracy, though he lacked definitive proof.

The pieces of the puzzle began to fall into place, forming a terrifying picture: not only had assassination attempts been made, but the criminal network had adapted after their failures. They hadn't stopped; instead, they had shifted to more subtle tactics, infiltrating his personal and professional life to break him from within. Eva, under their control, had become an instrument of psychological destabilization, while associates like Leander, under the guise of harmless intentions, could conceal far darker motives.

Realizing the depth of the conspiracy left Leo terrified yet resolute. He now knew the danger was real, pervasive, and that he needed to remain vigilant to outsmart this invisible network determined to destroy him. He found himself in a battle for survival, where every interaction could be a calculated move to ensnare him in a trap closing ever tighter.

As Leo began piecing together clues about the dark conspiracy looming over him, Eva, acting under Jürgen and the network's direct influence, subtly manipulated his doubts. When he expressed hesitations about Leander P., Eva firmly suggested he collaborate with the respected man, reminding Leo of Leander's impeccable reputation and influential position. She insisted that Leo's excessive suspicions were causing him to miss valuable opportunities.

Not only did Eva encourage this partnership, but she also insinuated that Leo's persistent concerns about Leander might be signs of a mental disorder. With calculated calm, she suggested the possibility of schizophrenia, exploiting his fears about his mental health to make him question his perceptions. She used this suggestion to reinforce the idea that he needed to stop distrusting everyone and instead embrace the alliance with Leander as a path to future success.

CHAPTER 3:

Eva: Both Victim and Accomplice

Eva, now central to the conspiracy to destroy Leo, found herself in a tragically complex position. She was both a victim of the criminal network, trapped and manipulated by Jürgen and his accomplices, and an unwitting accomplice in the gradual destruction of her husband. The contrast between her role as a victim and her actions as a complicit party added emotional and psychological depth to her character.

Eva had never intended to harm Leo. At first, her intentions were pure, and she loved him sincerely. But the schemes of the network, especially those of Jürgen, eventually broke her will. The master-slave dynamic that Jürgen had established rendered her completely submissive to his orders. Despite her humiliation and despair, Eva had lost control over her own life. She had become a tool in the hands of the criminal network, compelled to act against her will while fully aware of the harm she was causing.

The illusion of control she once believed she had in her toxic relationship with Jürgen had quickly shattered. He had not only seduced her but exploited her in the vilest ways, forcing her into relationships with other men under the constant threat of blackmail with compromising videos. The humiliations she endured extended beyond this: she was required to manipulate Leo, to alienate him from his children and loved ones, knowing all the while that she was complicit in his destruction.

Eva's deepest struggle lay in her sense of powerlessness. She saw herself as a puppet, yet each day she became more aware of her active role in Leo's suffering. The lies, the manipulations, and the psychological attacks orchestrated against her husband were actions she carried out despite the inner torment they caused. As events unfolded, she began to see herself as a traitor, incapable of escaping the web in which she was ensnared.

Deep down, Eva knew she could have resisted. There were moments when she nearly confessed everything to Leo, but fear paralyzed her. Jürgen and the network had isolated and enslaved her to such an extent that she convinced herself it was too late. Every step she took pushed her further away from the possibility of liberation. Her situation was that of a mental and emotional prisoner, desperately seeking a way to escape the mounting guilt that consumed her.

One of the most heartbreaking aspects of Eva's position was witnessing Leo's suffering firsthand, powerless to intervene. The network's orders were clear: she was to continue isolating him, driving him into depression or even suicide. The more she obeyed, the more she hated herself, yet she dared not defy Jürgen. The consequences of disobedience could be disastrous for both her and Leo, and she clung to the belief that her actions were, paradoxically, a form of protection for her family.

Despite her unwilling complicity, Eva remained a victim of circumstance. The criminal network had trapped her in a vicious cycle where every act of betrayal bound her more tightly to her manipulators. Leo, though still unaware of the full truth, increasingly sensed his wife's emotional distance without realizing she was both the instrument and the victim of a larger scheme.

In essence, Eva was caught in an emotional paradox. She was both responsible for her husband's suffering and powerless to free herself from the network's grip. Her dual role as victim and accomplice created an insurmountable inner conflict, plunging her into a spiral of guilt and despair while continuing her destructive actions under the network's pressure.

CHAPTER 4:

The Inevitable Confrontation

The confrontation between Leo and Eva, built up over months of secrets and unspoken tensions, escalated into a moment of raw and unexpected intensity. Exhausted by suspicions and the scattered evidence he had uncovered, Leo could no longer avoid facing Eva. This encounter was meant to put an end to the doubts that had been tormenting him, but he had no idea it would reveal much more than he expected, taking a far darker and more violent turn.

Leo approached the confrontation hoping for honest answers, a chance to understand what had led their relationship to become so toxic. However, the moment he voiced his suspicions, Eva adopted a hostile and disdainful stance. Instead of showing remorse or attempting to explain her actions, she attacked Leo outright, flipping the narrative and casting him as the one who had disrupted their relationship. Her gaze, once familiar and loving, turned cold and accusatory, and her tone became sharp and cutting, as though she was prepared to do anything to fend him off. She invited him to "leave," pointedly mentioning that "friends" were helping her now far more than he ever had, adding with a hint of arrogance that he no longer had a place there.

Stunned, Leo realized that Eva, far from being merely a victim of external pressures, had embraced her role in the conspiracy. Her loyalty now seemed firmly aligned with the "friends" she mentioned, mysterious figures whose names she withheld but who had apparently aided her in distancing herself from Leo, dismantling their marriage, and even viewing him as an adversary. This drastic shift in her demeanor was not just surprising to Leo; it was chilling. His wife had transformed from a silent accomplice to an active and menacing partner, ready to confront Leo to protect her new allegiances.

Desperate for answers, Leo pressed Eva about the identity of these "friends" and their intentions, but she provided no clarity. Instead, she allowed a sense of imminent danger to hang in the air, as though Leo should prepare for consequences simply for daring to confront her. She showed no trace of affection or attachment, making no effort to conceal her satisfaction at seeing him shaken. Her coldness and overt psychological aggression left

Leo staggered. The woman he had married, once gentle and loving, was now a stranger, openly threatening him with an implicit menace.

By the end of the confrontation, Leo came to a stark realization: he was no longer safe in his own home. Eva, who had once been his rock, had become a potential threat. She no longer hid her affiliation with a force bent on his destruction, and he understood the danger was not just real but immediate. This revelation marked a pivotal moment for Leo, who now recognized that the fight to preserve his life would not be merely psychological, it would also demand physical survival.

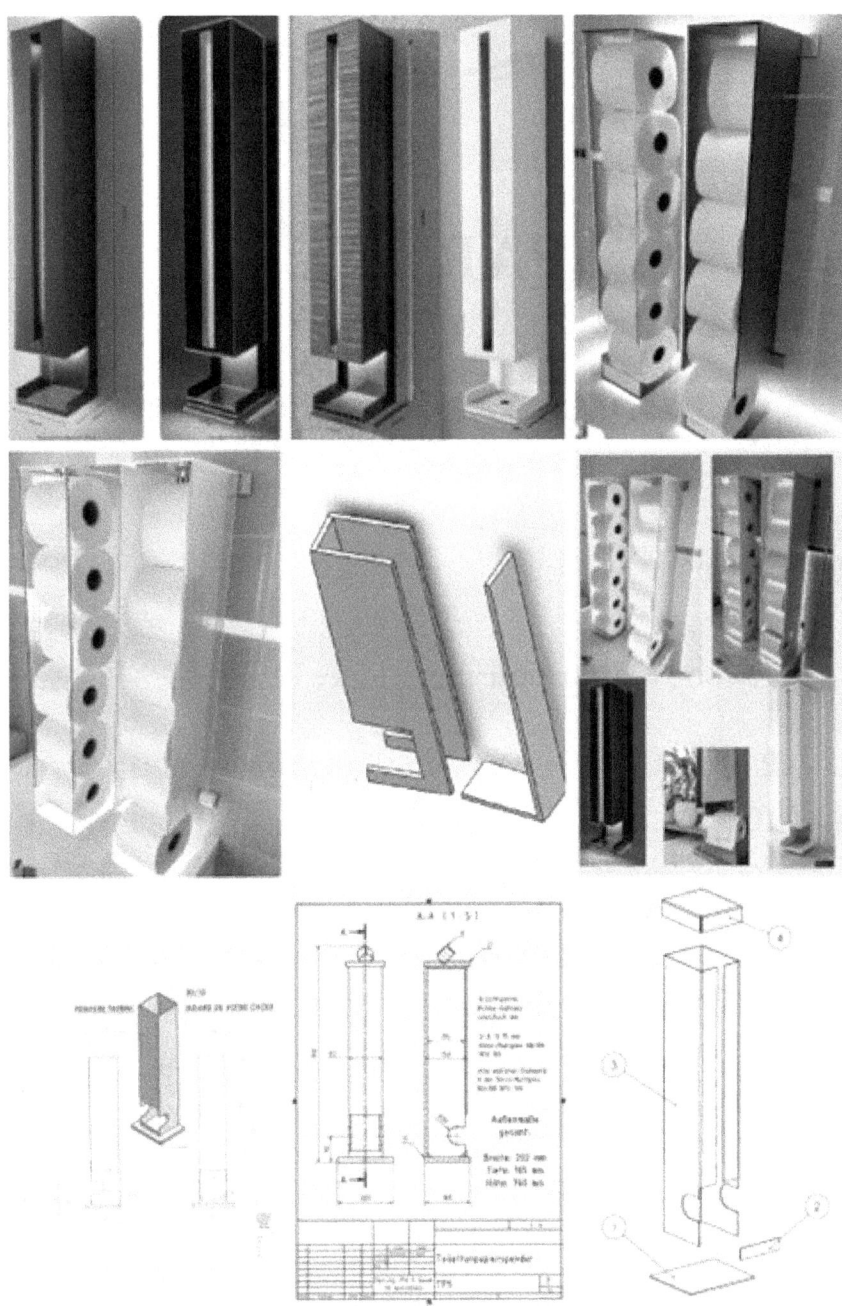

PART 12:

Devastating Truths

Chapters:

1. The Compromising Videos of Eva
2. Leo Confronted with the Ultimate Betrayal
3. The Combination of the Network's Destructive Interactions
4. Leo on the Brink of Collapse

CHAPTER 1:

The Compromising Videos of Eva

At this stage, Leo was still unaware of the existence of the videos that would shatter his life. Yet, he began to sense that something was gravely amiss, that his world was slowly crumbling beneath him. One Wednesday afternoon, while trying to call Eva, who was supposed to be at work, something devastating happened. Instead of hearing the familiar voice of his wife, Leo was met with muffled moans of pleasure, a woman's voice, and bursts of male laughter. Paralyzed, Leo remained silent, gripping his phone, unable to fully process what was unfolding.

As he listened in disbelief, he distinctly heard two male voices. One of them spoke about "getting a good shot," adding another layer of horror to Leo's anguish. The suspicion of infidelity he had long suppressed was confirmed in a moment as brutal as it was irrevocable. Leo was utterly crushed. This sudden phone call, a violent intrusion into his reality, left him completely unmoored. It was no longer a vague anxiety but an undeniable truth that struck with full force at his already fragile psyche.

Heart heavy and mind in turmoil, Leo waited for Eva to return home. When she walked through the door that evening, she found her husband in a pitiful psychological state, his face etched with exhaustion and pain. Without hesitation, Leo confronted her, demanding an explanation for what he had heard during the call. With chilling composure, Eva retorted that he was "crazy." She vehemently denied everything Leo described, accusing him of fabricating stories and losing his grip on reality.

Despite the glaring evidence, Leo found himself unable to hold her accusatory gaze for long. In what seemed like a calculated move, Eva headed to the kitchen and poured herself a large amount of alcohol. That day, she drank far more than usual, plunging her body and mind into an intoxicated haze. Afterward, she went into the shower, attempting to wash away the day's traces, and returned to their marital bed, where she began to touch herself provocatively.

Leo, shaken, watched her with a mixture of shock and disgust. He no longer knew how to interpret what he was witnessing. Eva, his wife, the woman he thought he knew, had transformed into someone unrecognizable. Her gestures, both careless and provocative, marked a turning point in their relationship. She no longer hid anything, exposing to Leo a world of depravity he could never have imagined being part of.

At that moment, Leo realized the woman he had loved was now unraveling before his eyes. She no longer tried to conceal her betrayal or lies but sank deeper into a self-destructive spiral, leaving her husband defenseless against her blatant disdain. Leo felt as though he was losing everything: his love, his dignity, and perhaps even his grasp on reality. But deep down, he still hadn't grasped the full picture. He didn't yet know that what he had overheard was only a fragment of a much darker reality, where compromising videos played a central role in the collapse of his marriage and life.

The revelations were yet to come, but for now, Leo remained trapped in denial, oscillating between the hope of reclaiming his wife and the certainty that he could never forgive what he had uncovered.

CHAPTER 2:

Leo Confronted with the Ultimate Betrayal

Leo was teetering on the brink of emotional and mental collapse. Clues had accumulated, Eva's behavior had grown increasingly strange, and despite multiple confrontations, he still lacked tangible proof of her infidelity or betrayal. However, the anxiety within him was mounting, and the suspicion that Eva was hiding something far graver was taking root.

One afternoon, Leo attempted to call Eva on her cellphone while she was supposedly at work. The phone rang, but there was no response. Instead, what he heard chilled him to the core. On the other end, there were sounds of moaning, mixed with male voices and a woman's apparent pleasure. The scene was confusing and profoundly traumatic for Leo. There were two distinct male voices, and one of them mentioned "getting a good shot." Stunned, Leo immediately hung up. He had not yet seen any compromising videos, but what he had just heard confirmed his worst fears: Eva was involved in something far more sordid than he had imagined.

This discovery shook Leo to his core. He was paralyzed, overwhelmed by pain and humiliation. That evening, when Eva returned home, Leo, in a state of utter despair, confronted her about what he had heard. He recounted the call, the voices, the sounds. But Eva, without hesitation, snapped back sharply: "You're crazy. You're making things up." She turned the tables, insisting that Leo was losing his mind, becoming more paranoid, and imagining things that didn't exist.

That evening, after throwing these accusations at Leo, Eva began drinking heavily, a habit she had recently adopted to drown her own torment. Leo, hoping for a moment of honesty, found only disdain and denial. Eva took a shower and then returned to the marital bed, where she began to touch herself, a habit she had recently taken up, which left Leo deeply disturbed and disoriented. He watched as his wife spiraled into erratic behavior, yet he still couldn't understand why she was acting this way.

However, the truth, still unknown to Leo, was far more terrifying. Eva wasn't merely unfaithful or manipulated by

Jürgen. She was trapped in a situation where her own life and the lives of their children were at stake. The criminal network, after ensnaring Eva in their web, had found an even more powerful lever to control her: her children. They made it clear that if she did not comply with their demands, they would release the compromising videos of her on private platforms and send them to authorities and social services. These videos, combined with Leo's declining mental state, would provide sufficient grounds for social services to remove the children from Eva and Leo's care, placing them in foster systems.

These systems, supposedly safe, would in reality become prime hunting grounds for the criminal network, which knew how to exploit the vulnerabilities of children under state protection. For Eva, the message was clear: cooperate or lose her children. Faced with this unbearable threat, she chose to fully submit, not out of a simple desire to betray Leo, but from a maternal instinct to protect her children. Leo had no idea that the network's manipulations had reached such a degree of cruelty.

From that point on, Eva played an increasingly active role, not only in her own humiliation but also in Leo's destruction. She no longer had control over her life; she had become a puppet of the network, forced to follow their orders to the letter to safeguard her children. Her strange behavior and destructive actions toward Leo weren't driven solely by malice or betrayal but by a deep and visceral fear of the consequences if she refused to cooperate. Eva was both a victim and a complicit party, trapped in a macabre game from which she saw no escape.

Leo, on the other hand, though increasingly suspicious that something terrible was unfolding, remained ignorant of the sordid manipulation. He felt betrayed, but he did not yet have access to the full truth. Each day, he lost himself further in the labyrinth of his suspicions and pain, unable to discern his wife's true motivations, let alone grasp the full extent of the threat looming over him and his family.

The ultimate betrayal was not simply that of an unfaithful wife but of a network willing to do anything to destroy a man, using his own family as a weapon. Leo was now utterly alone, besieged on all sides, unable to see any light at the end of the tunnel.

CHAPTER 3:

The Combination of the Network's Destructive Interactions

The criminal network, aiming to perfect its plan of destruction against Leo, realized that relying solely on Eva's manipulation would not be enough to guarantee their success. To maximize their control over Leo, they decided to introduce another person into his close circle, an agent who could observe him closely, influence his decisions, and report any signs of resistance or doubt. This new agent, carefully chosen to avoid arousing suspicion, was Leander P., the millionaire.

Leander P. enjoyed a respectable reputation as an influential businessman and engineer. With his skills, wealth, and power, he appeared to be an ideal ally for Leo, himself an accomplished engineer. Leander began to draw closer to Leo, not just to establish business ties but to closely monitor his reactions to the various pressures being exerted on him.

Leander had visited Leo several times, particularly in his office. During each encounter, he urged Leo to abandon his personal projects and join his enterprises for what he called "fruitful and promising collaborations." On the surface, it seemed like a generous offer, but Leo had no idea that behind this proposition lay one of the key pieces of the conspiracy orchestrated against him. Leander P., far more than just a businessman, was one of the masterminds behind the criminal network.

The initial interactions with Leo were subtle. Leander aimed to create an atmosphere of trust and professional exchange, hoping that Leo would eventually abandon his own projects. However, as Leo resisted these attempts at manipulation, Leander began to intensify his efforts, seeking to infiltrate Leo's life further to better control his actions and anticipate his responses.

It was no longer just about influencing Leo; it was about constantly monitoring him and reporting every detail of his behavior, conversations, and even emotional states back to the network. Leander, operating from the shadows, played the role of a master spy. He led a double life, appearing to be a mentor and potential ally to Leo while secretly executing a sinister plan to destroy him.

Each visit to Leo's office served two purposes: to convince him to give up his professional ambitions and to steer him toward a path that would make him more vulnerable to psychological control. Leander knew full well that by refusing to join him, Leo would become easier to isolate, a man alone against forces he did not yet understand.

At the same time, Leander strengthened the network's grip by relaying valuable information about Leo's mental state, his growing doubts, and his struggle to comprehend what was happening around him. To ensure total control, Leander devised a calculated strategy that, while flattering Leo's professional skills, dangled promises of mutual success. In reality, this was merely an attempt to exert greater control and maintain constant surveillance over Leo.

The irony was that Leo, due to Leander's influential position in the business world, had no reason to suspect that this seemingly benevolent man was part of the plot to destroy him. Leander concealed his true intentions well, appearing to Leo as a potential supporter. Burdened by failed assassination attempts and Eva's manipulation, Leo had not anticipated that this man, whose true motives were unknown to him, was playing a critical role in his descent into despair.

This dynamic between Leander and Eva, two pawns of the network, was designed to maintain tight surveillance over Leo and ensure that every attempt to destroy him, whether psychological or physical, would not fail. Together, they represented two facets of a complex conspiracy, with Leo simultaneously influenced from within by Eva and monitored from the outside by Leander.

CHAPTER 4:

Leo on the Brink of Collapse

Leo, drained by the series of traumatic events and still under the grip of the criminal network, remained oblivious to Leander P.'s true intentions. Yet, in his growing despair, he began to consider collaborating with him. A cursory investigation into Leander revealed no suspicious background, no ties to extremist ideologies or a Nazi past, which temporarily reassured Leo that this partnership might provide a way out.

This illusion of safety was precisely what the network exploited. For such subtle and destructive missions, they employed individuals who appeared impeccable, public figures or respected businessmen, to disguise the true purpose of their operations. Leander P., a successful engineer like Leo, presented a friendly demeanor and enticing business proposals. To Leo, he symbolized an escape from the increasing chaos in his personal life.

In his fragile psychological state, Leo was desperate to escape the mounting problems in his personal life. Eva, once his most trusted ally, had turned cold, distant, and manipulative. His home was no longer a refuge but a constant source of pain. In this context, Leo decided to accept Leander's outstretched hand, convinced that this partnership could offer him a fresh start professionally and ease his troubled mind.

But this decision would seal his fate.

What Leo did not know was that Leander and Eva were both connected through the same criminal network. Their shared objective was clear: to destroy Leo, mentally, emotionally, and financially. The partnership Leander proposed was nothing more than a ruse, a carefully orchestrated trap to draw Leo deeper into a tightening web. Now, Leo was not only enduring Eva's manipulations in his private life but also becoming prey to Leander's schemes in his professional sphere.

Leander P., with his influence and resources, began to manipulate Leo's professional decisions. He persuaded Leo to abandon his innovative projects and focus on collaborations that appeared lucrative but were, in reality, designed to undermine his previous successes. Mentally weakened by the relentless attacks from those around him, Leo failed to see through the deception. To him, Leander represented a source of support during a crisis.

At every step of the partnership, Leo felt an increasing discomfort. His business endeavors seemed to slip through his fingers, and he found himself making decisions he would never have considered before. The network now controlled every facet of his life: Eva played the role of emotional saboteur at home, while Leander orchestrated Leo's professional downfall. This dual assault, on personal and professional fronts, left Leo feeling increasingly isolated and powerless.

As his business began to crumble under Leander's influence, Leo lost the little control he had left over his life. One by one, his projects were abandoned, and each day, he felt his vision, creativity, and resolve dissolving in a haze of doubt and manipulation. What was supposed to be a lifeline turned into another tool for the network to dismantle his life.

Leo, unable to distinguish friends from foes, sank deeper into an abyss. He struggled desperately to maintain control, but each attempt failed, exacerbating his plight. He still could not grasp that all the events unfolding around him were part of a meticulously orchestrated plot, spearheaded by Leander P. and Eva, two seemingly opposite figures, united in their mission to destroy him.

The trap had closed around Leo, both at home and in the workplace.

PART 13:

The Fall of Leo

Chapters:

1. Leo Facing His Mental Destruction
2. Eva, Torn Between Guilt and Submission
3. A Relationship Shattered Forever
4. The Choice Between Vengeance and Despair

CHAPTER 1:

Leo Facing His Mental Destruction

Leo, caught in a web of manipulations orchestrated by Eva on an emotional level and by Leander P. on a professional level, felt his mind deteriorate a little more each day. Initially, the attacks seemed fragmented: Eva destabilized him at home through subtle manipulations, while Leander P. posed as a well-meaning business partner with destructive intentions. It didn't take long for Leo to realize that these actions were perfectly coordinated.

Leander's role in Leo's downfall was central, albeit insidious. Under the guise of professional collaboration, he set seemingly harmless traps that aimed to ruin Leo's reputation, career, and ultimately his entire life. Leo had enthusiastically entered the partnership, believing it to be a way to overcome his financial difficulties and regain control of his business. But after two months, none of Leander's promises had materialized. Leo hadn't received any income, and every attempt to address the payment delays was met with flimsy excuses. Leander blamed administrative errors, technical issues, and banking delays. The truth was, he never intended to pay Leo anything.

In reality, Leo was sinking financially without immediately realizing it. The network, through Leander, had meticulously orchestrated his collapse. Leander played the role of a "benevolent partner," but behind the scenes, he manipulated every detail to weaken Leo. The pinnacle of this strategy came during a financial crisis for Leo when Leander dared to offer him a "loan." For a man like Leo, accustomed to success, the prospect of relying on someone whose honesty he still believed in was humiliating. This offer, disguised as help, was nothing less than a calculated blow to destroy what remained of his dignity.

Leander didn't stop there. He pushed the manipulation further by placing Leo in compromising situations. On several occasions, he left large sums of money lying around in the company's conference room, hoping that Leo, desperate in his financial situation, would give in to temptation and take some of it. This would provide the perfect excuse to accuse Leo of dishonesty. The network sought to exploit Leo's every weakness, and Leander was an expert at staging such traps.

The height of this strategy came when one of Leander's mistresses, fluent in Leo's native language, was introduced into the equation. Leander asked Leo to act as a translator, pretending he needed help negotiating with her. This woman, acting under Leander's orders, was tasked with attempting to coax Leo into conspiring against Leander. This would provide Leander with solid grounds to publicly accuse Leo of dishonesty and completely destroy him.

Leo, still internally battling his confusion and disoriented by the events, began doubting his own judgments. He wanted to believe that his partnership with Leander P. was his way out. In reality, it was part of a more extensive and twisted plan. The network had woven its web relentlessly: Eva was emotionally destroying him at home, while Leander P. ruined him professionally and financially. They worked in perfect synchronization, with clearly defined roles in this scheme designed to break Leo on every front of his life.

Unable to understand why everything around him was falling apart, Leo watched as his world crumbled. The accumulation of Eva's manipulations at home, Leander's refusal to pay him, and the attempts to trap him at work all pushed him closer to the edge. The idea of resisting and surviving became increasingly blurred, leaving Leo imprisoned in a situation where he had lost all control. What he had perceived as a chance for redemption was nothing more than a sophisticated trap leading him inevitably toward total destruction.

CHAPTER 2:

Eva, Torn Between Guilt and Submission

Eva was now trapped in a hellish spiral of guilt and total submission, a prisoner of a network that controlled every aspect of her life. Guilt consumed her from within. She had never intended to harm Leo, her husband, but the pressures exerted by Jürgen and the criminal network had gradually eroded her resistance. She had become their slave, incapable of making decisions not dictated by fear or threat. The weight of betrayal bore heavily upon her, and though she was aware of the pain she inflicted on Leo, she could no longer free herself.

Every day, Eva oscillated between the shame of her submission to Jürgen, who manipulated her with cruel subtlety, and the terror of the repercussions if she tried to rebel against this oppressive system. The network's threat against her children kept her in a constant state of submission. They knew that targeting her children was the most effective way to control her. By threatening to expose her compromising videos, the network tightened its grip, making her understand that her children would be taken by social services and placed in centers where they would become easy prey. This fear paralyzed her.

Despite her desire to protect Leo, Eva knew that any attempt at rebellion would backfire on her. Jürgen, her ruthless master, didn't hesitate to humiliate her, delivering her to other men and even women to satisfy their fantasies, a reality she endured with pain and resignation. Their relationship had become one of master and slave, with Eva entirely subject to his desires and orders, devoid of any hope for escape. Jürgen owned her completely. Even when she tried to resist or regain some semblance of control over her life, he would brutally remind her of her place, wielding constant threats to keep her under his thumb.

The situation grew increasingly unbearable. Eva suffered not only from the guilt that gnawed at her but also from the disgust she felt toward herself. She saw herself destroying the man she had once loved, dragging him into a hell orchestrated by criminals who held her life in their hands. This duality, her love for Leo and her submission to the network, consumed her, plunging her into deep despair.

Despite it all, she continued to obey, following orders. Each psychological manipulation she inflicted on Leo brought her closer to the ultimate betrayal, yet she no longer knew how to stop the process. She saw clearly that Leo was suffering more and more, losing himself in his own confusion, but she was equally trapped. The network had succeeded in turning her into a puppet, unable to escape this destructive cycle.

Deep down, Eva still hoped for a way out, a miracle that would free her from this submission and allow Leo to understand her situation. But this hope seemed increasingly unlikely, and each day brought her closer to her ultimate downfall, where guilt and submission would completely destroy her.

CHAPTER 3:

Relationship Shattered Forever

Leo's relationship with Eva, once filled with love and complicity, was now reduced to ruins. He knew that his wife was no longer his own. She was merely a puppet obeying the orders of another man, Jürgen, and his criminal network. This transformation, both brutal and gradual, had entirely redefined their bond. Leo, who had always been strong and resilient, now saw his wife not as a victim to be saved but as a complicit player in a plot designed to destroy him.

Eva, on her end, no longer hid her intentions. She wanted Leo out of the house, making it clear that he no longer belonged there. She openly asked him to find another place to live, far from her and the children. These words, another form of betrayal, struck Leo with unimaginable force. The man who had given everything for his family now found himself rejected and betrayed by the person he loved most. Eva openly communicated with other men, signaling a definitive rupture in their marriage. Not only did she no longer hide it, but she almost flaunted her new loyalties with arrogance.

Leo, once an imposing figure standing 1.95 meters tall and weighing 105 kilograms, had lost 30 kilograms in just a few months. This drastic weight loss reflected his deteriorating mental and physical state. He now subsisted on nothing but black coffee, without sugar. His diet had dwindled to the bare minimum: he could go three days without eating, and when he did, it was merely a piece of cheese or a barely touched fruit. Food brought him no comfort, nor did any other daily activity.

The stress and accumulated pain robbed him of sleep. He spent entire nights staring at the ceiling or replaying in his mind the moments when everything began to fall apart. Forty-eight hours could pass without him closing his eyes, and even when he managed to fall asleep, his dreams were plagued by nightmares where Eva and Jürgen appeared, orchestrating his downfall. This chronic insomnia and lack of nourishment weakened him more and more each day, not only physically but mentally. He was becoming a shadow of himself, unable to comprehend how everything had spiraled so drastically out of control.

Eva, on the other hand, appeared increasingly detached and disconnected from their shared life. She had chosen a different side, that of Jürgen and the criminal network. Leo could no longer deny that his wife was under the influence of forces beyond his grasp and that she no longer saw him as her husband. Their marriage was now merely a façade, a remnant of what had once been a strong bond but was now irreparable.

Through her increasingly cold interactions, Leo saw clearly that their relationship was doomed. The criminal network had not only infiltrated his professional life but had also destroyed what he held most dear: his family. Despair began to overtake him. He felt trapped in a downward spiral where every attempt to understand or reconcile only worsened the situation.

This dynamic, where Eva no longer hid her actions and Leo was systematically demeaned, created a toxic atmosphere with unbearable tension. Every word exchanged, every glance was laden with reproach, unspoken truths, and accumulated suffering. Eva no longer made any effort to hide her affairs or parallel activities, and Leo no longer had the energy or desire to confront her.

The house they once shared, a symbol of their union and family, had become nothing more than a prison for Leo, a place ruled by betrayal and pain. With each passing day, he watched his world crumble further, along with the last shred of dignity and stability he was desperately trying to hold onto.

This situation only deepened the network's grip on Leo, who, emotionally isolated, physically weakened, and psychologically destroyed, found himself at the mercy of the dark forces seeking his ruin. The relationship between Leo and Eva, once built on love and respect, was now irreparably broken, with no hope of redemption.

CHAPTER 4:

The Choice Between Vengeance and Despair

Faced with the collapse of everything he had built, Leo found himself at a mental and emotional crossroads. On one side was the crushing weight of despair, urging him to abandon all struggle, and on the other, the lure of cold vengeance against those who had destroyed him. This choice was not merely an emotional one but a matter of survival. For Leo, it was an internal battle of monumental proportions, between giving up and fighting back.

Leo had lost not only his dignity and self-confidence but also his connection with his children, who had been manipulated by Eva and the network. His once-rational and brilliant mind was unraveling under the constant pressure of psychological manipulation, Eva's lies, and his professional failures. Each day, he was confronted with relentless reminders of his downfall.

Despair loomed as a natural response to a situation that seemed impossible to escape.

He thought about his children, the pain they would feel if he disappeared from their lives for good. This fragile bond with them, although distorted by Eva's lies, tethered him to a semblance of reality, a reason to live. Yet the temptation to leave everything behind and succumb to the psychological weight grew increasingly enticing. Leo knew that if he didn't act quickly, he risked losing himself entirely to the despair consuming him more each day.

However, the idea of vengeance haunted Leo. The humiliation of being manipulated by Eva, betrayed by his friend Leander P., and ensnared in a web of lies spun by a criminal network stirred a deep-seated rage. He wanted revenge against everyone who had turned his life into a living hell. But how could he achieve it in his physically, emotionally, and mentally weakened state?

Leo knew that vengeance required strength he was no longer certain he possessed. It demanded patience, strategy, and the ability to turn situations to his advantage. Yet the thought of striking back against the oppressive forces gave him a reason to hold on. He reflected on every manipulation, every lie that had contributed to his downfall. Each moment of his unraveling presented an opportunity for calculated revenge.

The criminal network hadn't just destroyed his personal and professional life, they had humiliated him and stripped him of his humanity. Leo realized that to rebuild himself, he needed to summon a new kind of strength, one driven as much by justice as by vengeance. But could he fight back without losing himself in the process? Vengeance offered a chance to reclaim his life and break free from the chains of the network's control, but it also risked leading him down a darker, more destructive path.

As he revisited the months of mental torture and manipulation, Leo considered different ways to exact revenge without jeopardizing his children's safety. He knew that acting impulsively could cost him everything. Yet despair, with its promise of immediate release, remained an alluring escape. It was a cruel dilemma.

Eva, now almost a stranger, was no longer an obstacle. Leo understood that their relationship was over, irreparably shattered by betrayal. He saw her as part of the machinery that had facilitated his downfall, even though she was also a victim. But this reality, a woman enslaved by the network's will, did nothing to ease his pain. Could he truly forgive her? Or should he, instead, include her in his plans for revenge?

The duality between vengeance and despair now defined his existence. While vengeance offered a glimmer of hope for personal redemption, it risked plunging Leo deeper into a spiral of violence and hatred that could destroy him even further. Despair, while seductive in its promise of immediate peace, meant abandoning his identity and everything he had been.

The battle was now raging in his mind. Leo had to choose, and quickly.

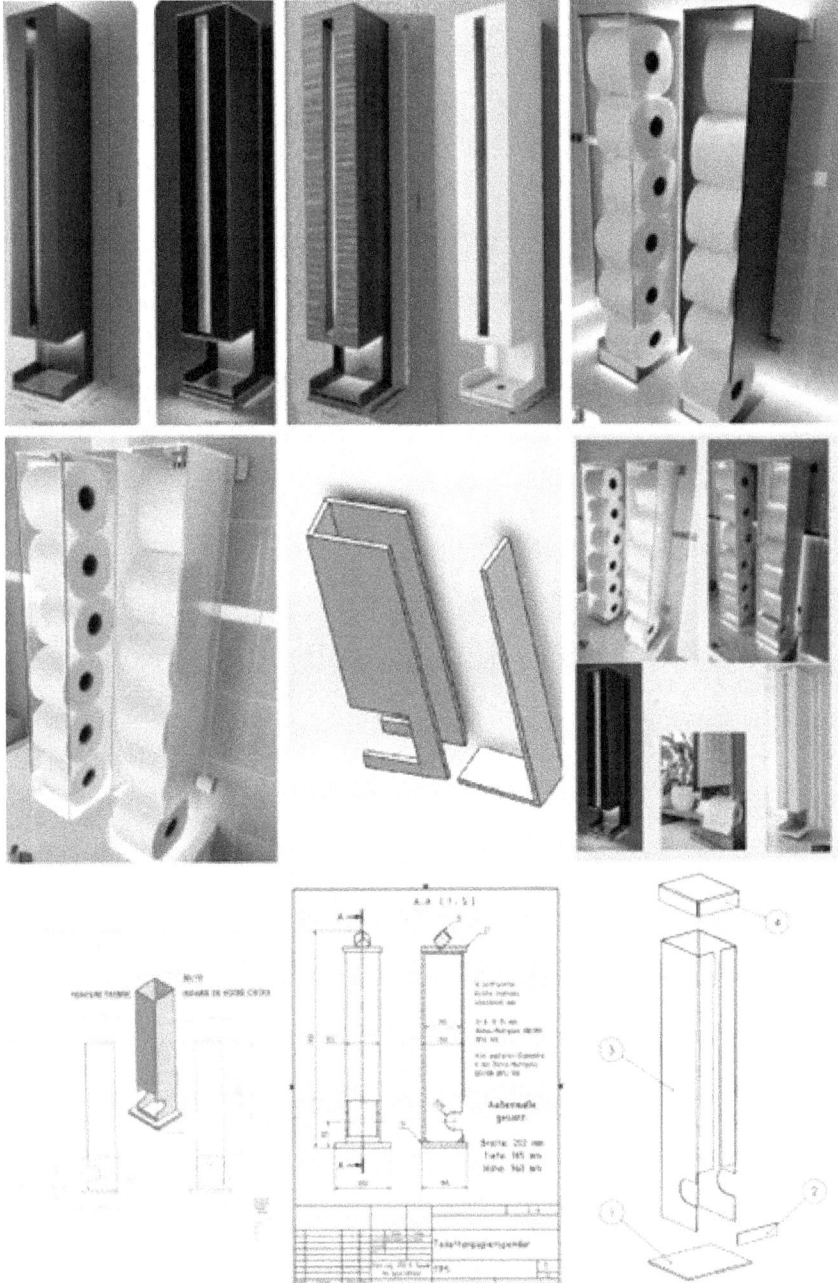

PART 14:

The Manipulators Exposed

Chapters:

1. The true masterminds behind the conspiracy

2. The criminal network revealed

3. Eva was just a puppet

4. The quest for justice or revenge

CHAPTER 1:

The true masterminds behind the conspiracy

The veil was slowly lifting for Leo, but what he uncovered shook him more than he could have imagined. The clues he had pieced together revealed that the conspiracy against him went far beyond business rivalries or conventional power plays. He now saw shadowy figures, faces of those lurking in the higher echelons of power, pulling the strings of his downfall. These shadowy figures, powerful and influential in business and politics, exposed through their actions and rhetoric a deeply ingrained dimension of systemic racism. To them, Leo was far more than a professional obstacle; he was an intruder, a foreigner who had dared to believe in the promise of a Germany where merit led to prosperity.

This concept, the "German Dream," which he had long cherished, now crumbled before his eyes as an inaccessible myth.

Unlike the American ideal, where social mobility was almost celebrated regardless of origins, the Germany he now discovered seemed resolutely closed, hermetically sealed, and ready to do anything to maintain a status quo in which the elite never opened its doors. The German elite, to which Leo had naively imagined he could belong, or at least integrate, was now unequivocally closed to him.

This bitter reality became evident through whispered conversations, avoided glances during meetings, and his increasing invisibility. Leo now noticed murmurs, allusions to his "origins," and stares questioning his belonging to a world where he clearly did not fit. Those orchestrating the conspiracy, men and women in powerful, untouchable positions, influential in political and economic circles, used their power not only to exclude him from spheres of success but also to tarnish his image and reputation with deeply ingrained prejudices. Leo realized he was not just a rival; he had become a symbol of what this closed society rejected.

Every attempt to recover, every effort to prove his legitimacy, seemed doomed to failure. Leo was targeted not only for what he had achieved but for what he represented: a challenge to the unspoken rules of their society. He began to see that even his business contacts, men like him, who had come from afar but were driven by the same dream, were distancing themselves, discouraged by a system willing to do anything to uphold this veiled segregation. Those he thought were close, colleagues and friends with whom he had built his career, gradually pulled away, influenced by rumors deliberately spread by his enemies.

For Leo, each day became a struggle against this harsh reality. These powerful figures, like an invisible circle around him, made him an example, a silent warning to others like him: Do not try to succeed here. This is not your place.

The "German Dream" as a Forbidden Myth

The masterminds of this network saw Leo, as someone not born in Germany, as an intruder in a system they believed was reserved for a select group of natives. This ideology was rooted in the concept of cultural exceptionalism, which, in this context, became an excuse to sabotage any social or economic advancement of individuals of foreign origin. Unlike the myth of the "American Dream," where social mobility is broadly encouraged regardless of origins (at least in theory), the "German Dream" seemed to remain inaccessible, an invisible but unyielding barrier for those outside the traditional elite.

The orchestrators of the conspiracy exploited latent racism within institutions and social circles to erode Leo's position. Rumors were spread, insinuating that his successes were "illegitimate" or "undeserved" because he was not of German origin. This stigmatization became part of a carefully orchestrated smear campaign, playing on deeply rooted prejudices in certain strata of society, where the success of non-Germans was seen as a threat.

To the true orchestrators of the plot, Leo was an anomaly in a society they wanted to keep closed and homogeneous. One key figure in the network, for instance, could belong to an old family of German industrialists and view Leo as a threat to the "purity" of the national entrepreneurial elite. This figure would use their influence not only to sabotage Leo's business ventures but also to reinforce in the media and professional circles the idea that Germany was not a place for the social ascension of foreigners, furthering a message of cultural segregation.

Leo gradually came to understand that his fight had become symbolic and that he was being used as a cautionary example for other foreigners who might have believed in total integration and deserved success. The orchestrators of the plot used him to set a precedent, implicitly reminding others that success remained a reserved privilege.

This revelation plunged Leo into a broader understanding of his struggle. It was no longer just about saving his career and honor but about fighting against an entire system designed to exclude and marginalize.

CHAPTER 2:

The criminal network revealed

As Leo delved deeper into his clandestine investigation, an unsettling and intricate portrait of the criminal network controlling every aspect of his downfall emerged. This was no stereotypical band of petty criminals or media-sensationalized mafias; it was a chillingly sophisticated organization rooted in the upper echelons of German power. Operating in the shadows, their actions reverberated with a silent brutality that destroyed lives, careers, and dreams without a shred of remorse.

As Leo unraveled the mysteries of the network that had ensnared him, he uncovered an even darker facet of this organization. It wasn't merely a group of individuals seeking to enrich themselves or expand their influence; they had developed a level of criminal sophistication that combined state-like authority with mafia-esque practices. This unique blend of power and psychological terror formed a frighteningly effective approach, one rooted in the perfected science of subjugation from the East German regime: Zersetzung.

Zersetzung, a method honed by the East German secret police (Stasi), wasn't about physical elimination. It aimed to mentally and psychologically dismantle its targets, to erode their relationships, careers, and sense of self until they had no sources of support left. Much like during the GDR regime, these methods sought to erase all traces of independence or resistance, but now employed modern tools.

The masters of this network co-opted state machinery for criminal ends, turning officials and agents into cogs in their machine of destruction. Illegal wiretapping, systematic surveillance, and administrative manipulations were just some of the tools Leo discovered, all inspired by the shadowy techniques of the past and adapted to the modern age of communication and information control. It became clear to him why every attempt at escape, even symbolic, had failed: his entire existence was under scrutiny. Every relationship was monitored, every movement anticipated.

Leo began to see why this operation was so relentless. He wasn't merely a threat; he had become a symbolic target, a silent warning to others who, like him, might dare to believe in the possibility of a future outside the self-proclaimed elite of this society. In this context, what they cynically called the "German Dream" was nothing more than a carefully maintained illusion to obscure the realities of power.

The more these revelations piled up, the graver Leo realized his situation was. This wasn't just a plot to ruin him, it was a meticulously crafted plan to destroy him from the inside out, using the very resources of the state. And knowing how effective Zersetzung had been in the past, Leo understood that only a surge of willpower could save him from succumbing to the insidious terror surrounding him.

Leo now saw that his plight was no accident: he was the target of a finely tuned machine, a pawn to be crushed in a chess game where he didn't even know the rules.

This realization filled him with both helplessness and anger. He was alone, with no one to turn to, trapped in a web from which he couldn't tell if he could ever escape. But one truth now burned in his mind: if he wanted to survive, he had to confront the network, expose their schemes, and shatter their influence, even if it meant putting his own life at risk.

CHAPTER 3:

Eva was just a puppet

As Leo uncovered the secrets that had destroyed his life, a chilling truth emerged: Eva, far from being a willing accomplice, had never been more than a pawn in the hands of a far more powerful criminal network. Exploiting her naivety and vulnerabilities, the network had ensnared her in a web of manipulation, stripping her of agency and reducing her to submission. Like countless other women drawn into this trap through false promises and hopes, Eva had been nothing more than an instrument, a victim whose innocence and flaws served as bait for those pulling the strings from the shadows.

The extent of the network's manipulation didn't end with Eva. Leo discovered that other women had suffered similar fates. These women, often educated and full of promise, were carefully targeted, each carrying a painful and hidden story. Among these silent victims was a doctor Leo met years after his ordeal. Her testimony of her own descent into darkness, so eerily similar to Eva's, shook Leo to his core. Her words revealed the psychological devastation these criminal organizations inflicted, infiltrating the lives of intelligent, independent women who unknowingly became puppets.

The doctor's story, with its striking parallels to Eva's, left Leo reeling. She described the subtle threats and gradually imposed demands, the escalation of tasks, and the isolation that followed. Like Eva, she had started with seemingly harmless "small favors," only to find herself ensnared in a web of lies and forced acts. Years later, she still couldn't find peace, haunted by the memory of having served a system whose evil she only fully understood after it had broken her. Leo realized that Eva's plight was not unique; she was one of many victims of this silent network, which preyed on their fears and vulnerabilities.

The network's methods were insidious and calculated. Women like Eva, the doctor, and even promising students were drawn into a spiral of manipulation. Those who resisted or tried to escape faced the gravest consequences, including death threats. In extreme cases, students with bright futures were lured into questionable opportunities, only to disappear or be silenced. The brutality of the orchestrators became glaringly evident to Leo, filling him with boundless rage and sorrow as he grasped the scale of the scheme that had ensnared his wife and countless others.

As Leo pieced together Eva's past, he saw that she too had endured phases of fear, isolation, and blackmail. At first, she had tried to hide her involvement, but over time, she became increasingly submissive, eventually losing the ability to make decisions independently. This network, blending state-like omnipresence with mafia-style coercion, relied on a method called Zersetzung, a psychological annihilation strategy originating from East Germany's secret police (Stasi). Once used to destroy dissidents, this technique had been taken to the extreme, eroding victims' autonomy and self-confidence, leaving them entirely under the control of their masters.

Eva's story took on a tragic and cruel dimension for Leo: every action she had taken under the network's control, every word, every manipulation, had been engineered not only to break him but also to destroy her. Eva, once full of life, had become a shadow of her former self, a ghost trapped in a nightmare not of her making. Leo, overwhelmed by this reality, no longer knew whether to hate her for what she had done or pity her for what she had endured. The image of his wife now appeared to him as that of a prisoner, stripped of her dignity and freedom.

Amid this revelation, Leo realized that his mission could not stop at freeing himself from the chains of this conspiracy. He felt compelled to seek justice for Eva and all the others who had been crushed by this organization. His anger transformed into a cold and relentless determination: he had to dismantle the network, expose those who manipulated and destroyed lives from the shadows, and finally shatter the cycle of suffering orchestrated by unseen hands.

CHAPTER 4:

The quest for justice or revenge

For Leo, the next step was far from a simple decision, it was a point of no return, an internal transformation spurred by the monstrous truths he had uncovered about the criminal network that had ravaged his life and the lives of so many innocent people. Faced with these revelations, Leo found himself torn between two equally complex and critical paths: the pursuit of justice, with its inherent limitations and adherence to the law, or the path of vengeance, where he could strike directly at those who had methodically orchestrated this destruction.

As Leo wrestled with this decision, a deep disgust took hold of him for the impunity these criminals enjoyed. The system, designed to protect the innocent, seemed fragile and powerless in this context. This insidious network, entrenched in every stratum of power, manipulated the very institutions meant to deliver justice. Their crimes, hidden behind respectable facades and institutional complicity, made the pursuit of justice slow, uncertain, and often illusory. Victims like Eva and the countless other women ensnared in their schemes were numerous, but their stories remained silenced.

Leo realized that traditional justice, with its endless procedures and often insufficient evidence, might turn out to be a dead end. To achieve justice, he would have to fight within a biased system, where every element could be weaponized against him by those in power. Abandoning this path, however, would go against his deepest values. Could he truly forsake the pursuit of justice and become judge and executioner himself? Could he plunge into the shadows to strike mercilessly, knowing it might cost him the last remnants of his humanity?

On the other hand, vengeance exerted a dark allure. The idea of confronting those who had destroyed his life, exposing them, and forcing them to face their crimes felt cathartic, almost necessary. But this path was fraught with danger: it could quickly drag him into a spiral of violence where he would become little more than an instrument of rage. In seeking vengeance, justice would no longer be an end in itself but a means of restoring his dignity. Yet, Leo knew that vengeance would not bring him true peace and that he risked losing himself entirely in an unending war against enemies who thrived in the shadows.

Leo's reflections led him to consider a hybrid strategy, one that would allow him to retain his integrity while striking at the network with precision and relentlessness. Instead of engaging in direct confrontation, he could gather evidence to publicly expose the organization's activities, use his skills to infiltrate their operations covertly, and make their system vulnerable from within. Leo saw this approach as a way to combine justice and vengeance: dismantling the network not through outright violence but by exposing their crimes, destabilizing their operations, and awakening public awareness.

For Leo, the path was fraught with uncertainty, but fear no longer held him back. His pursuit of justice or vengeance was no longer about easing his pain, it was about freeing those, like Eva, who were still imprisoned by this web of manipulation. Leo understood that every action, every strategy, had to be meticulously planned. His fight was no longer merely personal; it became the fight of all the victims who had never been able to find peace.

With this resolution, Leo moved forward, determined to fight without betraying the principles that defined him as a person. His battle would be long, but he was ready to face it, no matter the cost.

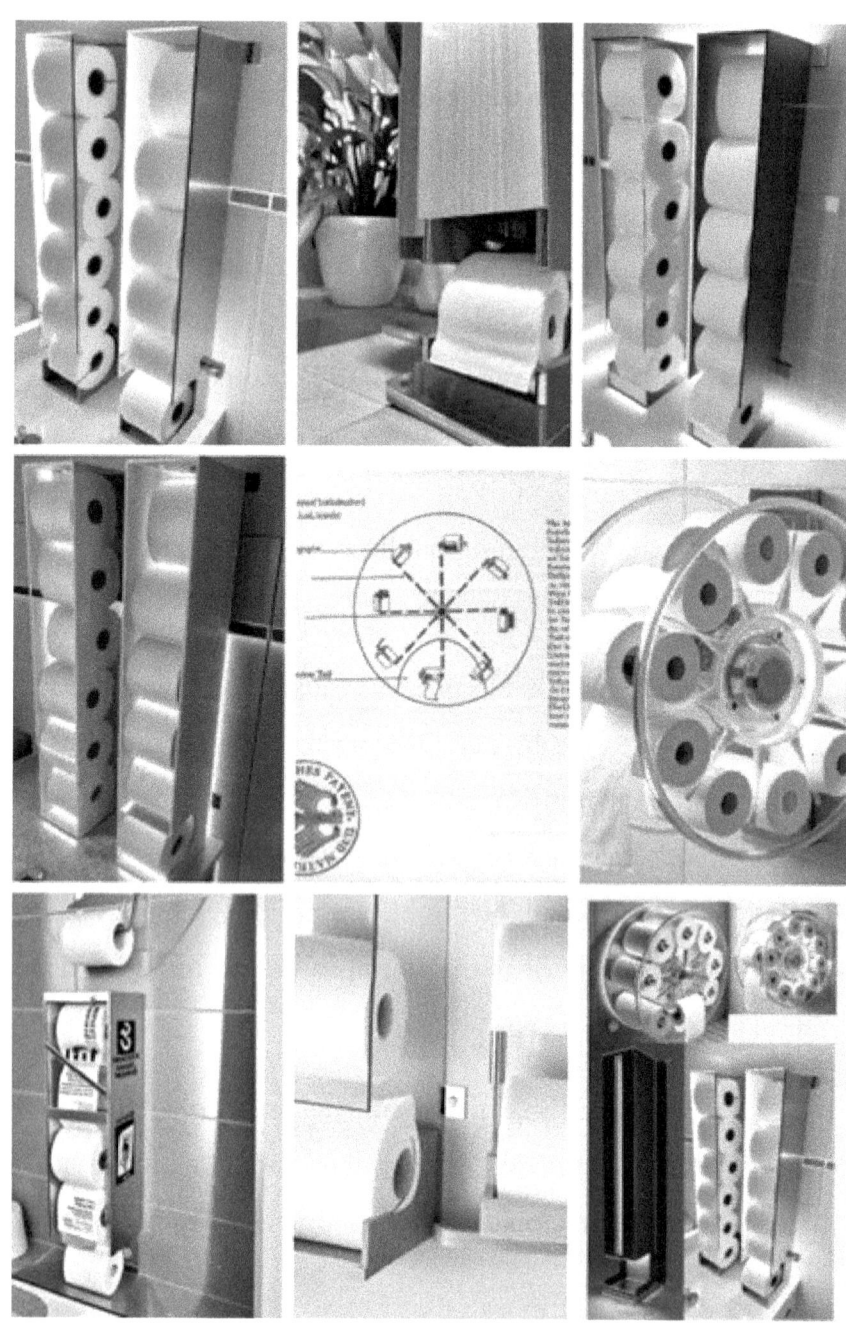

PART 15:

The Final Revelation

Chapters:

1. The discovery of the final elements of the conspiracy

2. The invisible ramifications

3. Leo faces his destiny

4. The ultimate choice

CHAPTER 1:

The discovery of the final elements of the conspiracy

As Leo progressed in his personal investigation, he uncovered another, even more disturbing revelation that exposed the brutality of the criminal network. Beyond psychological and financial manipulations and attempts on his life disguised as accidents, Leo discovered that he was also the target of invisible attacks aimed directly at his physical health.

The network was not content with destroying Leo mentally and emotionally; they also targeted his body. Leo realized he had been exposed to silent weapons such as microwaves and lasers, used to gradually degrade his health without leaving visible traces. He noted unusual symptoms, such as extreme fatigue, severe migraines, and unexplained bodily pains, which he suspected were linked to these targeted attacks.

Delving deeper into his research, Leo discovered that two apartments had been rented in close proximity to his own, with layouts that allowed the network to target him discreetly. One of these apartments, which he had assumed was unoccupied, was in fact being used by Jürgen, the "Romeo Agent," to maintain his grip on Eva and monitor Leo's every move. This close surveillance enabled them to inflict physiological damage while observing his reactions and amplifying psychological pressure.

The effects on Leo's health were devastating. The microwave and laser attacks had direct consequences on his physical resilience, leading to rapid weight loss and chronic sleep problems. The combination of these invisible assaults and constant manipulations from those around him weakened him further. Leo realized he was not just a victim of psychological manipulation but also of systematic physical destruction.

What he did not yet know was that the network had also set ambushes along his daily routes. Network members positioned themselves at specific points to discreetly attack him using these technologies. Initially unable to understand why his health was deteriorating so rapidly, Leo finally discovered that these attacks were part of a meticulously orchestrated plan to destroy him on all fronts.

These revelations profoundly shook Leo, who realized the network would stop at nothing to annihilate him, not just psychologically and socially, but physically as well. His home, which he had thought was his only refuge, was no longer a safe haven but a hunting ground for these criminals. He understood that every aspect of his life had been infiltrated, leaving him defenseless against these invisible assaults.

Confronted with this new discovery, Leo faced a dual threat: he was ensnared by the psychological manipulation of his wife and the professional schemes of Leander P., while also being physically targeted by a network intent on his total destruction. These elements, uncovered late in his struggle, opened Leo's eyes to the scale of the conspiracy against him, a plot meticulously designed to engulf him in an abyss of suffering with no escape.

Leo now knew he had to act, but he felt more isolated and vulnerable than ever.

CHAPTER 2:

The invisible ramifications

As Leo delved deeper into the layers of the criminal network that had entangled and dismantled his life, he uncovered a chilling truth about its scope and malice. What he was experiencing was not unique. Leo realized that others before him had fallen prey to these shadowy networks, enduring similarly devastating manipulations. Among these cases, the story of Gustl Mollath stood out, a man whose tragic fate mirrored Leo's in disturbing ways.

Gustl Mollath, a whistleblower who exposed tax fraud within a major German bank, became ensnared by an influential network determined to silence him. Following his revelations, he was falsely accused of violence and deemed dangerous, leading to his forced psychiatric commitment for seven years. Mollath fell victim to a system that, in protecting powerful financial and economic interests, labeled a man of integrity as mentally unstable and hazardous. His ordeal bore a haunting resemblance to Leo's struggle.

One of the most harrowing aspects of Mollath's case was the role of his wife. Similar to Eva in Leo's life, Mollath's wife was weaponized by the network to facilitate his downfall. She was manipulated into fabricating allegations against her husband, accusing him of domestic violence. Though baseless, these claims were used to justify his institutionalization, serving the network's goal of silencing him. Like Leo, Mollath faced a life shattered by intimate betrayal orchestrated by forces far beyond his control.

The parallels between Leo's plight and Mollath's were unmistakable. Just as Mollath's wife had been turned into an instrument against him, Eva had been actively involved, used as a pawn by the network to destabilize Leo from within. Leo began to understand that the destruction of his mental and emotional well-being was intricately linked to this indirect manipulation. These networks didn't merely seek to eliminate their targets physically; they aimed to break their spirits by exploiting those they loved most.

Using spouses and close relationships to exert intense psychological pressure was a common tactic among such criminal networks. This recurring pattern, evident in both

Mollath's and Leo's cases, underscored how these organizations ruthlessly exploited emotional vulnerabilities to achieve their objectives. For Leo, this realization marked a turning point in his understanding of the intricate and far-reaching conspiracy targeting him.

As he unraveled the manipulations affecting his life and those of others like Gustl Mollath, Leo recognized that his case was just one piece of a much larger puzzle. The network he faced was not limited to his immediate surroundings, it extended into broader spheres, infiltrating judicial, law enforcement, and even medical institutions.

The network, as Leo now understood, didn't operate solely in the shadows. It had infiltrated key sectors of society: judges, police officers, bureaucrats, and influential business figures were all implicated to varying degrees. Some were ensnared, others willingly corrupt, and still others acted out of fear for their families, facing threats similar to those imposed on Leo.

The way corrupt police officers used their positions to report Leo abroad without legal justification, based on fabricated accusations, showcased the network's immense power. Leo realized he was the target of a system far larger than himself, caught in a web that reached far beyond personal vendettas. This network wasn't simply intent on destroying him, it sought to maintain control over all it could touch through illicit and clandestine means, sometimes even leveraging state resources.

The ramifications stretched further still. Leo discovered that the network's reach extended across national borders. His movements abroad were meticulously monitored and flagged, not by official channels, but by corrupt individuals within German police forces who used their power to ensure Leo was treated as a pariah even in foreign countries. This kind of network operated with sophisticated tools and connections spanning multiple nations, explaining why Leo, despite attempts to distance himself or seek refuge elsewhere, found himself trapped in an unrelenting cycle of oppression and surveillance.

This wasn't merely a matter of personal vengeance. Leo realized that the stakes were much higher. The network he faced wasn't just trying to destroy one man, it sought to uphold a system where anyone challenging its interests would be systematically crushed. Its invisible tendrils reached into both public and private institutions, and every action against Leo was designed to leave him powerless, ensuring he could never recover.

Leo now faced a grim truth: he wasn't just fighting for his survival, he was battling a vast and merciless machine that had already claimed countless other victims.

The invisible ramifications of the criminal schemes targeting Leo became increasingly evident. This network, like the one that had destroyed Gustl Mollath's life, operated with terrifying precision, employing not only physical but also emotional and psychological destruction. The connections between Leo's case and Mollath's were no coincidence. These networks had mastered the art of exploiting the most intimate human relationships to manipulate and obliterate their targets.

CHAPTER 3:

Leo faces his destiny

Leo stood at the climax of his ordeal, caught between resignation and confrontation. After uncovering the full extent of the criminal network's machinations that had dismantled his personal and professional life, he was overwhelmed by feelings of powerlessness and solitude. His struggle had grown into something far beyond what he had imagined, and he realized he was no longer merely a victim but a central figure in a game of power that extended beyond his own existence.

Leo now saw himself as a man at the mercy of forces intent on annihilating him, both physically and mentally. The grip of his enemies had infiltrated every sphere of his life: professionally, with Leander P.'s betrayal and sabotage of his business ventures; personally, with Eva's betrayal under Jürgen's control, leaving him alone to face his worst nightmares; and even physiologically, through covert methods like microwave weapons and subtle poisoning that affected his health. Every aspect of his being had been systematically corroded by a network with boundless resources and destructive ingenuity.

Confronted with this onslaught of suffering, Leo wondered if he had the strength to fight back. As he reflected on the betrayals he had endured and the recent revelations he had uncovered, he found himself at a crossroads: Should he seek vengeance, delivering justice on his terms, or retreat, broken, in a desperate attempt to preserve what little remained of his life?

Leo's destiny was embodied in this existential dilemma: He could pursue the path of vengeance, embarking on a destructive crusade against those who had orchestrated his downfall, risking becoming a shadow of his former self. Alternatively, he could take the harder path of resilience, seeking justice not through violence but by exposing the crimes and attempting to rebuild his life from the ruins.

For Leo, every decision came at a cost. He knew that going after the network might endanger his own life and that of his children. Yet accepting his fate without fighting back could mean the complete erasure of his existence, his integrity, and everything he had built. He began to consider legal action to expose the conspiracy, though the corruption within the police and judicial institutions left him with little hope for an easy victory.

This ultimate choice, between total collapse or a fierce fight for redemption, haunted Leo in the days following his discoveries. The mental pressure became unbearable, and he realized he could no longer afford to evade reality. If he chose to fight, he had to accept that victory would not come easily and that he might lose even more along the way.

Thus, Leo found himself in a profound inner struggle. He was both a man broken by circumstances and one who, in moments of despair, sought a glimmer of hope to transform his pain into strength. His fate remained uncertain, but his decision would determine whether he succumbed to complete destruction or chose to rebuild himself, even if it meant starting from nothing.

CHAPTER 4:

The ultimate choice

As Leo faced the collapse of his life, he stood before a crucial decision that would determine his future. He knew that directly confronting the criminal network would be futile; their power, resources, and influence were too vast. However, Leo refused to be a passive victim of this corrupt system. He decided to arm himself with a different strategy: the power of public and international opinion.

Leo understood that the only way to destabilize this powerful network was to expose their existence to the world. He aimed to prove that, in modern Germany, heinous crimes such as attempted assassinations, psychological torture, and systematic manipulations were being carried out illegally, and worse, with taxpayer money. By appealing to international public opinion, he hoped to draw the attention of human rights organizations, international media, and even supranational judicial bodies like the European Court of Human Rights.

The battle he was fighting was not just a personal struggle against the network but a state scandal. Leo began compiling all the evidence he had gathered, recordings, anonymous letters, clues about the assassination attempts, and manipulations, and planned to use them as weapons to alert public opinion. He understood that only by exposing these methods could he highlight the flaws in the German system, where certain authorities, including the police, had collaborated with criminals with impunity.

His personal investigation led him to delve deeper into Zersetzung, an old psychological demolition technique used by the Stasi, the secret police of East Germany (GDR). Leo discovered that this method was more than just mental manipulation. Zersetzung (literally "decomposition" or "erosion") was a criminal science taught at the Stasi academy in Potsdam. It had been used to destroy political opponents in the GDR, not by physical elimination but by subtly and often invisibly ruining their lives.

Zersetzung targeted individuals' mental and social well-being. It sought to isolate the target, destabilize their daily environment, and destroy their personal and professional relationships while creating an atmosphere of distrust around them. This manifested in smear campaigns, psychological manipulations, and even sabotage in the smallest details of daily life. It was precisely what Leo was experiencing, and he now understood that this weapon, once wielded by a totalitarian regime, had been adopted by modern criminal networks, a fusion of mafia tactics and corruption within parts of the German police.

The network targeting Leo used this science of psychological destruction to annihilate individuals like him, not through brute force but through subtle, relentless attacks designed to break them mentally. By exposing these practices, Leo hoped to reveal that these oppressive techniques, inherited from the authoritarian GDR regime, persisted in contemporary Germany, illegally and often with the complicity of authorities.

At this point, Leo knew that his survival depended on his ability to expose these crimes. The ultimate choice he faced was not merely one of vengeance against his enemies but of uncovering the truth. He chose to fight, no longer solely for himself but for all those who were victims or could become victims of this criminal system lurking in the shadows. His struggle transformed from a personal battle into a universal fight for justice, with the hope of breaking the network's influence and ending these outdated methods.

Leo knew this path was perilous and that his enemies would likely try to eliminate him before he could make too much noise. But he was willing to take that risk. He understood that his survival, and that of other victims, depended on bringing everything into the light: public denunciation, media exposure, and international pressure. He hoped that this path would not only liberate him but also protect his children and prevent other lives from being destroyed by the same network.

Thus, Leo chose not to succumb to blind vengeance. He opted to expose the network's crimes, fight for the truth, and denounce these mafia-like methods operating with impunity under the guise of legality. This ultimate choice, justice, became his sole means of redemption and his only path to inner peace.

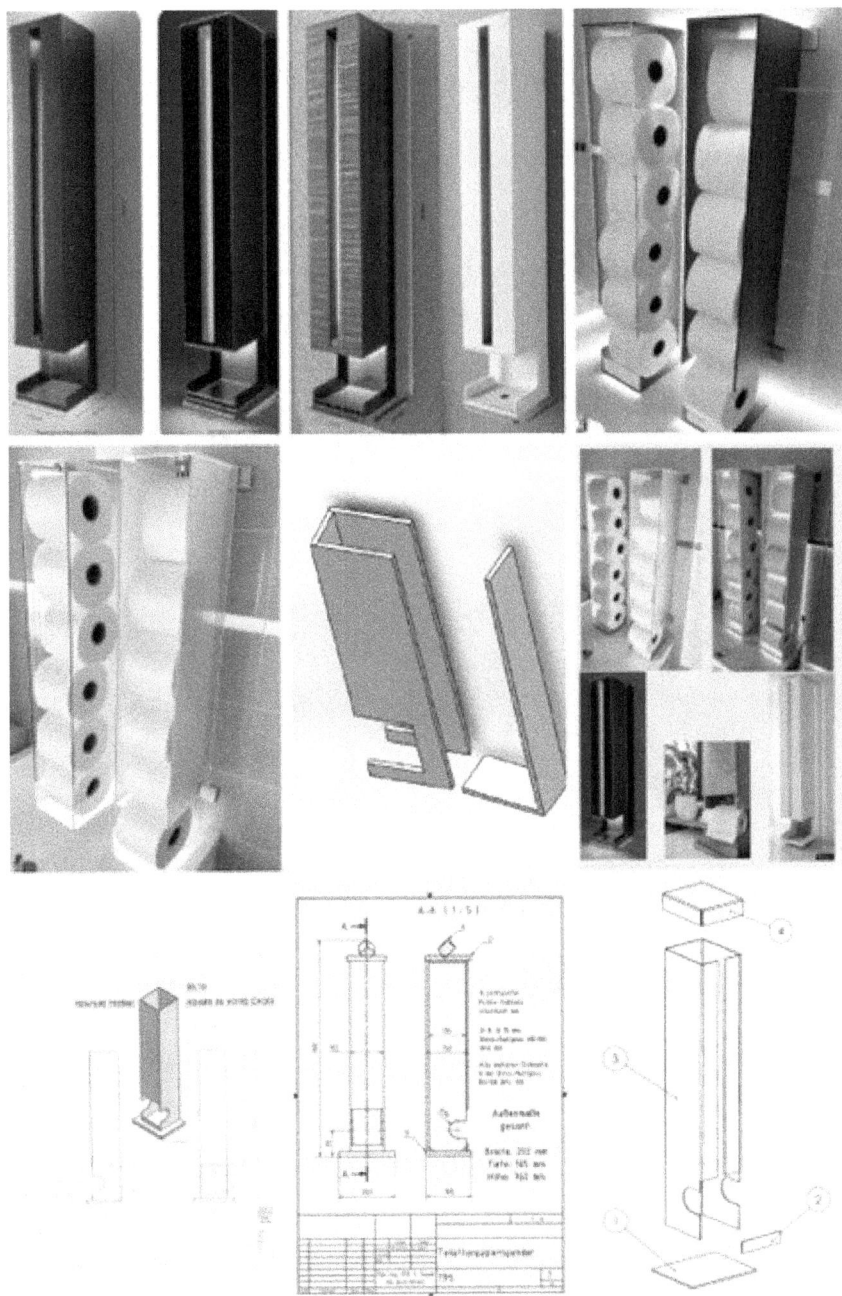

PART 16:

On the Ruins of Truth

Chapters:

1. Leo After the Storm

2. Eva, a Broken but Freed Woman

3. Surviving the Horror of Truth

4. The Uncertainty of the Future

CHAPTER 1:

Leo After the Storm

After enduring a storm of manipulations, betrayals, and attempts at psychological destruction, Leo found himself at a pivotal point in his life, trying to rebuild. The aftermath, however, was far from an immediate period of peace. Instead, it was marked by an intense internal struggle as he grappled with the consequences of what he had endured. Leo had lost much: his emotional stability, his family connections, and even his confidence in himself.

One of the most unsettling aspects of this post-crisis period was the profound loneliness. Leo felt utterly isolated, not just because he had been estranged from those closest to him, but also because he now understood the full scope of the conspiracy against him. The chasm that had formed between him and Eva, his wife, had become unbridgeable. Though he knew she had been manipulated by the network and used as an instrument of his downfall, that knowledge did little to ease the sting of betrayal.

Leo realized that he had to learn to live alone again and redefine himself as an individual. His mental health had been severely impacted, and he understood that recovery would be neither easy nor quick. The effects of Zersetzung, the psychological destruction technique used against him, were still palpable. Once strong and self-assured, Leo now felt shattered by a method designed not only to undermine his mental health but also to dismantle his social and professional standing.

What made his reconstruction even more challenging was the realization that the authorities had played an active role in his isolation. He discovered that institutions meant to protect citizens had instead been complicit in his downfall. The criminal network had infiltrated not only his personal life but also co-opted state agents to ensure his complete marginalization. Leo grasped that this network didn't operate in isolation; it was bolstered by institutional support. This revelation deepened his despair, as he realized that even the systems he might have relied upon for justice were, in fact, corrupted.

A particularly painful chapter in this period was the enforced separation between Leo and his children. Under the network's influence, Eva had accepted a job 700 kilometers away from Berlin, a move seemingly encouraged by the authorities themselves. Leo quickly understood that this distance was not coincidental but part of the broader strategy to further isolate him. Being physically separated from his children was a calculated maneuver to sever his remaining emotional ties, making his situation all the more unbearable.

The manipulation by the authorities to facilitate Eva's relocation was not random. Leo realized that the network, increasingly aware of his growing understanding of their tactics, sought to neutralize him further. By keeping him physically apart from his children, they aimed not only to weaken him emotionally but also to reduce the likelihood of him thwarting their plans. The state apparatus, instead of upholding justice and protecting its citizens, had become an instrument of oppression against Leo. This added betrayal only deepened his anguish but also clarified the scope of what he was up against.

During this post-crisis period, Leo engaged in deep reflection. He delved into studying Zersetzung, the psychological weapon once employed by the Stasi in East Germany to dismantle political dissidents. This method, which systematically destroyed individuals without direct physical violence, was at the heart of what he had experienced. As a victim of this technique, Leo resolved to publicly denounce what had happened to him, aiming to expose the abuses perpetrated by a corrupted segment of the authorities.

Leo decided not to let himself be entirely destroyed. He saw international justice and public opinion as his last recourse. He knew he couldn't fight such a network alone head-on, but he could draw attention to his plight through the media and the international community. His strategy became clear: to expose the assassination attempts, psychological manipulations, and tortures he had endured, not only for his survival but also to protect others from falling victim to the same methods.

By shedding light on Zersetzung and revealing the role of corrupt state agents in his destruction, Leo hoped to safeguard his children and prevent others from being ensnared in the same traps. Though his body and mind were weakened, Leo refused to succumb to defeat. His mission to expose this criminal scheme became his driving force, a way to regain some semblance of control in a life that had been systematically sabotaged.

CHAPTER 2:

Eva, a Broken but Freed Woman

Despite appearances, Eva had never truly been freed from the grip of the criminal network. After the collapse of her relationship with Leo and her involvement in the manipulation orchestrated by Jürgen and his associates, Eva had been distanced from Leo, not to grant her freedom but as another means to control her. This geographical separation was a calculated strategy to prevent her from breaking down and revealing the truth. The network knew that if Eva remained close to Leo, the emotional pressure could eventually compel her to confess her role in their scheme. Isolated from Leo, she remained under the constant surveillance of the network.

Far from being liberated, Eva remained a tool of manipulation, a woman who, even without contact with Leo, continued to be exploited by those who had enslaved her. Jürgen and the network maintained their hold on her through relentless threats. Eva could not break free because she knew too much about their system and operations, making her a liability if she ever decided to talk. For this reason, they kept her under strict watch, using her whenever it suited their agenda.

Eva, shattered by years of manipulation and subjugation, was no longer the woman Leo had married. Her physical transformation bore the most evident testimony to her decline. Once a strong and vibrant individual, she had withered to a frail 52 kilograms, her body reshaped to conform to the preferences of those pulling the strings in the shadows. This drastic physical change was not merely a consequence of psychological pressure but a deliberate act by the network to mold her into the ideal profile desired by certain influential members of their criminal system. Over time, Eva had become a shadow of her former self. Her weight, calculated with precision, fit the exact physical standards sought by the network, which continued to exploit her for their hidden clientele. This transformation was not a natural fallout of events but a dictated outcome by the network, directed by Jürgen, to ensure Eva served as an instrument of their exploitation.

Thus, Eva remained a captive victim, not only of her past but also of the network that held total control over her. She was forced to comply with their demands and their model of domination. Any attempt she made to regain a semblance of normalcy was constantly undermined by this omnipresent manipulation. Through constant threats and pressures, the network ensured that she could neither speak out nor reclaim her life.

Eva had never escaped this web of control, blackmail, and manipulation. She was psychologically broken, enslaved for life, and reduced to a mere tool serving the interests of this destructive network. Eva was no longer a person but an object, a tool used at the whim of those who wielded absolute authority over her. Her existence was a series of horrors orchestrated by men who had seized total control of her body and mind.

Beyond her physical exploitation, the psychological grip was relentless. Eva knew that any attempt to escape would bring severe consequences, not just for her but for her children as well. The network was omnipresent, with every means necessary to destroy anyone who dared to defy them. They kept Eva captive through continuous threats, preying on her fears and guilt. She was acutely aware that she had played a role, willingly or not, in Leo's downfall. This burden on her conscience made her an easy target for manipulation, as she no longer saw herself as deserving of redemption.

Leo, meanwhile, had emerged from this nightmare deeply scarred, both psychologically and materially. Although he had survived the collapse of his life, he had never been part of the network. He had only ever been one of its primary victims. The network's ultimate goal had been to destroy him, using his own wife as a weapon against him, and they had succeeded in shattering his existence. What made the situation even more tragic was that Eva had been nothing more than a passive instrument, yet she remained forever tied to this system.

The control exerted over her had never loosened. Far from Leo, she was not free. On the contrary, the network had carefully orchestrated her removal to ensure she wouldn't crumble under the pressure and confess the truth. They knew that if she stayed near Leo, she might divulge all the details of the plot, compromising the network's integrity. By keeping her under their sway, they simultaneously protected her and maintained their grip on her. Eva had become their lifelong possession, a pawn they could use at will to satisfy their desires and agendas.

Despite the illusion of freedom, Eva remained a prisoner in her own body, unable to escape the hold of Jürgen and the other members of the network. This criminal system, deeply entrenched in society, had no intention of releasing her because she knew too much and posed a constant threat to their secrecy. As long as she lived, they would ensure she never spoke.

What had started with subtle manipulations and promises of freedom had devolved into an endless cycle of submission and control. Eva, broken by years of servitude, was now a lifelong captive of a network that used ruthless means to maintain its influence over its victims. Her physical, emotional, and psychological transformation was the direct result of the systematic oppression orchestrated by these criminals to solidify their power.

CHAPTER 3:

Surviving the Horror of Truth

Leo, after enduring a series of devastating trials, now faced a reality that haunted him daily. His once-thriving and stable life had been reduced to ruins by the machinations of a sprawling criminal network. Standing at a crossroads between vengeance and rebuilding, Leo found himself shaped by assassination attempts, Eva's betrayal, and the network's pervasive grip. Yet, far from collapsing, Leo turned this cruel truth into a new mission: to hunt down those who destroyed peaceful lives under the guise of cold anonymity.

Leo's quest for justice became deeply personal. Aware that his case was merely the tip of the iceberg, he discovered through his research that countless other victims had suffered similar orchestrated harassment and destruction. One striking parallel was the case of Gustl Mollath, a man unjustly institutionalized for years after exposing large-scale tax fraud within a German bank.

Like Leo, Mollath had endured the schemes of a system capable of crushing those who stood in its way. Mollath, who uncovered illicit financial practices, had been labeled mentally unstable, a strategy often employed to discredit whistleblowers. The criminal network targeting Leo deployed similar methods, leveraging the power and influence of corrupt authorities to silence dissenting voices.

But Leo's efforts extended beyond his personal ordeal. He took up the fight against these white-collar criminals who silently devastated lives and entire families. Central figures like Leander P. played pivotal roles in these crimes, supported by allies embedded at every level of institutional power. Armed with his discoveries, Leo realized their strength lay in fear, silence, and control, tools he vowed to counter with every resource at his disposal.

As his investigation deepened, Leo uncovered that the network's reach extended far beyond his case. Young women, particularly students, were another prime target of the network. Recruited through threats or seduction by so-called "Romeo Agents," they were drawn into prostitution and drug abuse. Those who resisted faced even graver consequences: infected agents would deliberately transmit viral diseases like HIV or hepatitis, condemning the women to shattered lives. Now aware of these horrific practices, Leo vowed to expose the full extent of these crimes in the next chapters of his story as he revealed more evidence of the network's operations.

Surviving the horror of the truth was not just about living with the past; for Leo, it was a daily battle. He did not merely nurse his wounds; he embarked on a personal war for justice. Eschewing blind vengeance, he chose to speak out publicly and expose those behind these criminal practices. His ultimate goal was to take his case to the international stage, proving that assassination attempts, psychological torture, and other crimes were being carried out in modern Germany, often funded by taxpayers' money. He delved deeply into researching a shadowy yet formidable technique once taught in East Germany: Zersetzung.

Zersetzung, a psychological tactic taught in the former East Germany, particularly in Potsdam, was designed to mentally destroy regime opponents without leaving a trace. These methods had survived the fall of the Berlin Wall and were now being used by mafias and corrupt factions within authorities. Determined to uncover the truth, Leo aimed to expose this criminal science, an invisible yet devastating weapon wielded by those who sought to maintain power through fear and intimidation.

By embracing this new mission, Leo displayed unwavering courage and determination. His suffering, far from consuming him, became the fuel for his rebellion against these unseen forces. He understood that he could not dismantle the entire network head-on, but he believed that his fight, amplified by public awareness, could alter the course of events. Surviving the horror of the truth thus became, for Leo, not just a personal struggle but a commitment to protecting others who, like him, risked falling prey to this destructive network.

CHAPTER 4:

The Uncertainty of the Future

After enduring so many trials, Leo was haunted by an even more troubling truth: the passive complicity of the German federal legislature in the actions of these criminal networks. Cases like his and Gustl Mollath's, though extreme, were not isolated anomalies. They illuminated a grim reality where criminal organizations operated with impunity, right under the authorities' noses, without any significant action being taken to stop them.

In his pursuit of justice, Leo confronted a crucial question: how could such crimes occur in a modern society under the surveillance of a structured state like Germany? The methods employed by these networks, psychological manipulation, blackmail, illegal reporting, and economic pressure, were not isolated or invisible acts. Their scale required sophisticated resources, often derived from intelligence services or state institutions. The silence of the authorities in the face of such crimes could not simply be a coincidence.

Leo began to understand that the passivity of the federal legislature in combating these networks suggested that the state might be indirectly complicit. In an era dominated by concerns over terrorism and advancements in intelligence technologies, it was difficult to imagine that activities of this magnitude, utilizing advanced technological means and involving an extensive network, could go unnoticed by security services. If the authorities were not responding, it was because they were deliberately turning a blind eye, either out of negligence or due to indirect ties with certain actors involved.

This realization led Leo to a bitter conclusion: through its silence and inaction, the state became complicit in the destruction of innocent lives. Families were torn apart, individuals like him and Mollath were hunted, defamed, and eliminated through covert means, yet no legislative reforms were forthcoming to curb this scourge. The system appeared designed to protect these mafia-like networks, which thrived under a legal framework that was either inadequate or intentionally permissive.

Thus, Leo realized that to survive the horror of the truth, he had to fight on multiple fronts: not only against the criminal network targeting him but also against a legislative and judicial system that was either corrupt or indifferent, allowing these crimes to persist in the shadows. He understood that his battle was far from over. The state's silence on these overtly organized crimes revealed that these actions were either tolerated or orchestrated by corrupt elements within public institutions.

In the face of this, Leo could no longer simply flee or strive to survive. He had to denounce these crimes on an international scale. He needed to expose not only his own case but also those of other victims of the network, ensuring the world understood that modern Germany harbored mafia-like systems that undermined the foundations of justice and democracy. Leo resolved to become a living witness to these atrocities, using every platform and support available to shed light on the extent of the crimes being perpetrated with the silent complicity of the state.

The road ahead was uncertain, but Leo now knew he was not just fighting for his survival. He was fighting to expose a hidden truth, to prevent others from enduring the same psychological and moral tortures, and to restore a semblance of justice in a world where injustice was tolerated by those who should be combating it.

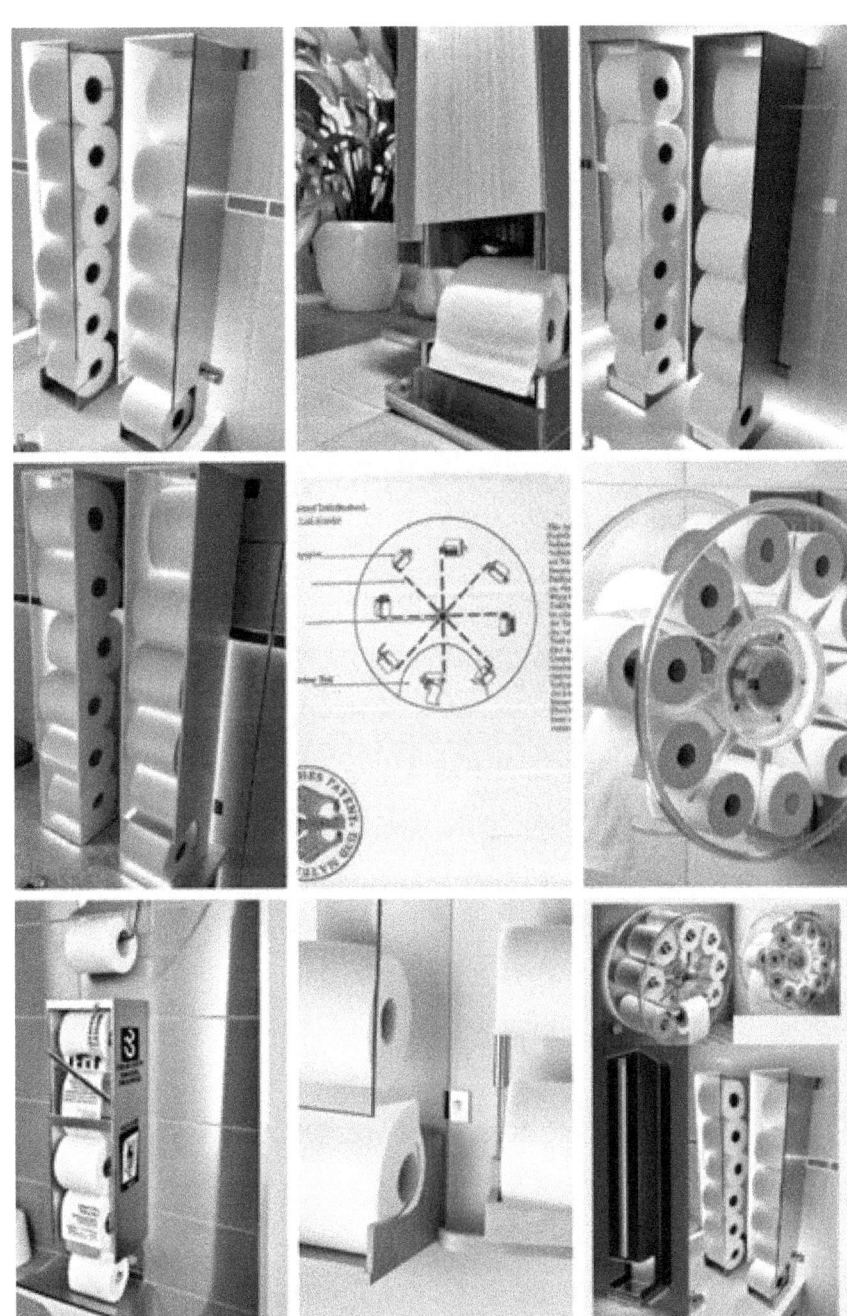

Epilogue

Biography of the Author

Wilfried S. Graf von Gerechtberg is a German legal consultant specializing in both French and German law as well as Germanic studies. In his work, he tackles a scourge afflicting Germany, amplified by the passivity of the authorities. Drawing inspiration from real events, he sheds light on organized crime employing methods such as digital weapons and Zersetzung, psychological torture tactics, reputation-damaging defamation, harassment, and more, rooted in practices from the former GDR.

Author's Note

Dear readers,

Thank you for following Leo's journey in the first volume of this misadventure, which portrays some of the grim realities and invisible threats making their way into our society unbeknownst to most. This novel stems from my desire to combat these criminal methods by raising public awareness about this phenomenon.

Synopsis for Volume II

This second volume delves into the practice of Zersetzung as applied to Leo, exploring its effects, other methodologies of destruction, and practical advice for victims or anyone seeking protection.

Zersetzung, a German term originating from the era of the Stasi in East Germany, refers to a method of psychological and social destruction of an individual. In Leo's story, it represents a sophisticated strategy designed to isolate, destabilize, and discredit its target, pushing them to question their own reality. This insidious approach manifests through subtle acts intended to be noticeable only to the victim, creating vulnerability and driving them toward a state of crisis.

Mechanisms of Zersetzung: Techniques of Daily Harassment

The strategies employed in this destructive method go beyond the capabilities of typical private organizations, requiring constant and discreet surveillance and harassment. These tactics involve funding subtle harassment campaigns where individuals shadow the victim, leaving traces of their presence that are too faint for external witnesses to confirm. The uniqueness of Zersetzung lies in its ability to maintain perpetual ambiguity: Leo notices unmistakable signs of surveillance, such as cars flashing their lights at the same time each morning and evening, but these cues remain too trivial for others to find suspicious.

The repetition of such seemingly minor incidents, like being photographed repeatedly by nearby individuals or noticing the same rental cars following him, fosters a growing sense of paranoia in the victim. Leo begins doubting his own perceptions, questioning whether he is truly being followed or if he is imagining the scenarios. This ambiguity is central to the goal of Zersetzung: to instill uncertainty in the victim's mind, leading them to defensive reactions perceived as excessive or inappropriate by those around them.

Volume II examines the psychological toll of these methods, providing an in-depth analysis of the strategies and their devastating effects, while offering guidance on recognizing, resisting, and mitigating the impacts of such manipulations. Through Leo's harrowing journey, this installment aims to empower readers with knowledge and resilience against the invisible forces of psychological warfare.

The Use of Public Resources and the Complicity of the Parallel State

The scale and logistics of such operations go far beyond the capabilities of an individual or private company. In Germany, the power of the state facilitates the use of significant resources for surveillance and harassment activities. These include the use of foreign license plates, often from Eastern European countries, or vehicles from complicit companies. Some of these companies and institutions are linked to the Reichsbürger network, a movement comprised of individuals who reject the authority of the Federal Republic of Germany and dispute its legitimacy. Although they appear to be dissidents, these individuals are embedded within society, occupying roles in administrative services, education, security, healthcare, and private security firms.

The Reichsbürger network benefits from a certain level of impunity in its actions, particularly in providing logistical support for harassment campaigns like those targeting Leo. They become ideal allies for the Zersetzung network, offering services, vehicles, and infrastructures beyond the scrutiny of ordinary citizens. This corrupted influence allows them to bypass the limitations of the state, using its resources to finance operations with dark and destructive objectives.

Psychological Manipulation and Forced Institutionalization

A primary goal of these actions is to provoke the victim into irrational behavior. Leo, subjected to relentless harassment, reaches a phase of intense stress, where his reactions may seem exaggerated or paranoid to those around him. For individuals not experiencing these daily micro-aggressions, his responses appear disproportionate. This biased perception is amplified by the network's accomplices, who exploit Leo's emotional vulnerabilities to generate widespread misunderstanding and, in some cases, label him as mentally unstable.

This is where Zersetzung demonstrates its full destructive potential. Using its influence, the network manipulates health professionals, particularly psychiatrists, who are either complicit or directly involved. These professionals employ biased diagnoses to further destabilize the victim. Isolated from his support system, Leo can then be institutionalized under false pretenses of mental illness. This tactic, while not new, was a core element of the Stasi's psychological manipulation strategies, where psychiatrists were often tools in a system that crushed individuals under the guise of "treatment."

Women Victims: Partners Trapped in an Invisible Network

Leo is not the only one suffering from this insidious Zersetzung. Many women also endure similar pressures and manipulations. These women, often naive or seeking stability, are exploited by the network for its own ends. Examples include Eva and others, students or professionals who are manipulated unknowingly and used as pawns in a larger game. Their complicity is often secured through blackmail or threats. Others, like a doctor Leo meets later, come to understand the network's reality and share their experiences to break the silence surrounding these practices.

Young and impressionable women are often manipulated into serving as intermediaries and agents of influence for targets like Leo. Those attempting to escape the network frequently face elimination, with their disappearances masked as accidents or suicides. Students or professionals who dare to speak out encounter smear campaigns that label them as delusional or paranoid, driving them into isolating despair. The psychological manipulation aims to break them while rendering them invisible to society.

Modernized Methods of Zersetzung: Advanced Manipulation from the RDA

The modern Zersetzung applied to Leo and others is an updated version of the Stasi's technique, enhanced by advanced technologies and criminal methods. Harassers do not merely follow or spy on their targets, they exercise comprehensive control through sophisticated technological surveillance, spyware, and concealed cameras. Technological advancements provide the network with new tools to maintain constant control, ensuring the victim remains in a perpetual state of fear and confusion.

These tactics are cowardly and criminal, chosen because the perpetrators cannot legally prosecute their victims, as they typically target honest, incorruptible individuals with clean criminal records.

The criminal actors behind this strategy combine state surveillance methods, mafia-style intimidation, and the psychological destruction strategies inherent to Zersetzung. Leo experiences not only physical harassment but also psychological torment, with every aspect of his life scrutinized, documented, and weaponized to deepen his insecurity. For instance, seemingly confidential information is subtly leaked, signaling to Leo that even his most private life is under surveillance.

The Ultimate Strategy: Breaking the Individual Without Direct Physical Violence

A defining characteristic of the Zersetzung targeting Leo is the absence of direct physical violence. Instead, the network relies on psychological and social violence to drive the victim to self-destruction. The ultimate aim is to irreparably break Leo, stripping him of any chance to return to a normal life. This insidious method involves maintaining absolute control over his existence, ensuring Leo remains isolated, misunderstood, and discredited in the eyes of society. To achieve this, the network invests in defamation, slander, and even uses coercion and violence against those who resist its commands.

Each act of harassment may seem insignificant on its own, but the cumulative effect becomes a devastating weapon. Through constant harassment, Leo is pushed into paranoia, losing confidence in himself and his perception of reality.

Zersetzung as applied to Leo is a strategy of psychological destruction where the goal is not to kill directly but to shatter the victim's mind first, hastening their demise without arousing suspicion. This is compounded by physiological deterioration caused by laser and microwave attacks aimed at compromising his health. This layered assault, combining psychological destruction and covert physical aggression, serves to accelerate the victim's breakdown, fulfilling the network's dark objectives.